Bijan Anjomi

美——彼尚·安裘密——著 米妮

我的天使 1

少年篇

Absolutely Effortless Prosperity For Youths

轻而易举的富足

云南出版集团
云南人民出版社

图书在版编目（CIP）数据

我的天使.1/（美）安裴密著；米妮.开开译. --
昆明：云南人民出版社，2015.12
ISBN 978-7-222-14233-6

Ⅰ.①我… Ⅱ.①安…②米…③开… Ⅲ.①儿童故事—美国—现代 Ⅳ.①I712.85

中国版本图书馆CIP数据核字(2015)第312314号
版权登记号：图字23-2016-002

出 品 人：刘大伟
责任编辑：朱海涛
出版统筹：杨柳Yana
封面设计：熊　琼
内文设计：7拾3号工作室
责任校对：黄　灿
责任印制：杨　立

我的天使1

[美]彼尚·安裴密　著　米妮　开开　译

出版	云南出版集团　云南人民出版社
发行	云南人民出版社
社址	昆明市环城西路609号
邮编	650034
网址	www.ynpph.com.cn
E-mail	ynrms@sina.com
开本	700mm×980mm　1/16
印张	16
字数	186千
版次	2015年12月第1版　2016年8月第2次印刷
印刷	小森印刷（北京）有限公司
书号	ISBN 978-7-222-14233-6
定价	45.00元

如有图书质量及相关问题请与我社联系
审校部电话：0871-64164626　印制科电话：0871-64191534

云南人民出版社公众微信号

献 词

我将这本书献给所有遍布这个星球的年轻朋友。
你们是美丽的,你们未来将成为完美的成年人。

玩吧,在生活中享受欢乐,
生活会带给你更多欢乐。

谢谢你们,
和我一起在这个星球上。
我爱你们!

两个或两个以上
生活在阳光里的孩子的力量
远远超过数以百计
活在黑暗中的人

目录 CONTENTS

引言 1

来自彼尚的信息 /3

如何使用此书 /4

故事 001

我和我的高级智慧就是这样开始连接的 /002

1·我观察我说了什么 /006
2·我留意我听到了什么 /008
3·我觉察我看到了什么 /010
4·我并不知道我所看见的真正意义 /012
5·我愿意看见光 /014
6·我警醒于光 /016
7·我非常富足 /018
8·每个人都希望为我贡献 /023
9·我值得富足 /025
10·我敞开接受宇宙所有的礼物 /027
11·我给予等同我接受 /030
12·我释放所有恐惧 /034
13·我敞开心扉走向和平 /037
14·我认出我的最佳利益 /040
15·我有耐心 /043
16·做出反应前,我暂停片刻 /046
17·我敞开接受奇迹 /049
18·我只选择和平 /052
19·我充满爱,值得被爱 /056
20·只有爱存在,恐惧是幻象 /060
21·父亲无条件地爱着我 /065
22·父亲爱我比我爱自己更多 /071

23・我信任我的父亲 /076
24・我父亲很伟大，我也是 /081
25・我放手，让父亲指引我 /086
26・作为宇宙之子，我是有福的 /089
27・今天属于我的高级智慧 /091
28・我在所有的事情里只看见爱和光 /095
29・我感谢一切 /101
30・我整天听到爱的声音 /104

奇迹日记 107

第一天・第一个故事 /108	第十六天・第十六个故事 /113
第二天・第二个故事 /108	第十七天・第十七个故事 /113
第三天・第三个故事 /108	第十八天・第十八个故事 /113
第四天・第四个故事 /109	第十九天・第十九个故事 /114
第五天・第五个故事 /109	第二十天・第二十个故事 /114
第六天・第六个故事 /109	第二十一天・第二十一个故事 /114
第七天・第七个故事 /110	第二十二天・第二十二个故事 /115
第八天・第八个故事 /110	第二十三天・第二十三个故事 /115
第九天・第九个故事 /110	第二十四天・第二十四个故事 /115
第十天・第十个故事 /111	第二十五天・第二十五个故事 /116
第十一天・第十一个故事 /111	第二十六天・第二十六个故事 /116
第十二天・第十二个故事 /111	第二十七天・第二十七个故事 /116
第十三天・第十三个故事 /112	第二十八天・第二十八个故事 /117
第十四天・第十四个故事 /112	第二十九天・第二十九个故事 /117
第十五天・第十五个故事 /112	第三十天・第三十个故事 /117

后记 118

引言

富足是有能力敞开心扉去接受宇宙赋予的所有礼物，那是我们存在的自然方式和天赐的财产。

富足的含义比有钱更丰盛，它还意味着完全的健康，无限的喜悦，完美的关系和全然的和平。

当孩子感觉到富足，他们知道他们值得拥有世界上所有美好的东西。

所以，他们可以放下那些局限和匮乏的信念系统，敞开心扉去迎接伟大的成功的未来——一个充满喜悦、和平和幸福的未来。

来自彼尚的信息

给我所有精彩的年轻朋友们：

你们是这个星球的未来。安驻在和平里，聆听你们的直觉，你们的高级智慧，还有你们的天使。

你不需要失去你家庭里的任何人来找到高级智慧，高级智慧已经在你体内，它将帮助你在每一个重要时刻做出最佳选择。

你最强有力的指导来自你的爸爸妈妈。请始终听从他们的建议，并一直记得——无论你是否看到，他们对你的爱比你能够想到的要多得多。只有当你有了自己的孩子时，才能体会到他们有多爱你。

我给你们所有最好的祝福，现在以及未来。

爱，光，和欢乐常在。

——你们的朋友，彼尚

如何使用此书

这三十个故事以《轻而易举的富足》第一册的功课为基础。这些故事让年轻的男孩儿女孩儿们触摸到他们自己纯真的美,并敞开接受他们自己,尊重热爱他们的父母,同时也尊重热爱这个星球上的每一个生命。

这本书设计的是每天一课,每日一个故事,故事的编号刚好与每月中的每一天相对应,如果这个月多了一天,你可以在这一天挑选一个你最喜欢的故事去读。

建议你在每天早晨醒来之后立即阅读当天的故事,晚上睡觉时再读一遍,从而带来快乐、喜悦和充满爱意的甜梦。思想关注什么,什么就会呈现出来,道理就是这么简单。这样做了,你的眼睛、头脑和心灵就会敞开迎接每一天、每一刻都有可能发生在你身上的奇迹。

然后,将你的想法和奇迹记录在书后的奇迹日记里,这会帮助你巩固每一天的功课,并使你自己更加敞开,看到生活中所有的奇迹。

每一天敞开接受并且认可这些喜悦、和平、爱、友谊、健康和丰盛的奇迹,并且和你的家人、朋友分享它们,三十天之后一定会出现最好的结果。

故事

当你心中充满爱时，恐惧就会消失，轻松和快乐就会到来

我和高级智慧就是这样开始连接的

这个家庭就像普通的家庭一样，充满爱的爸爸和妈妈，两个儿子，11 岁的盖博瑞和 10 岁的杰森。和其他的两兄弟一样，两个小男孩时常争论吵架。

一天早晨，男孩们正在争吵时，爸爸将他们拉到一边，问道："你们知道为什么你们总是争吵吗？"

杰森和盖博瑞同时指责对方偷了自己心爱的玩具，还抢夺好吃的食物。

爸爸听了一会儿说："不，那些不是你们争吵的真正原因。真正的原因是你们都忘了你们是谁，也忘了你们为什么来这儿。你们不记得你们在进入身体之前，对对方有着多么强烈的爱，所以你们才选择来到地球上成为兄弟，并且互相帮助。"

盖博瑞和杰森看了看对方，他们对这个说法微笑了。尽管他们不是很明白，但两个人还是认真地看着爸爸说："请再多告诉我们一些。"

爸爸和两个小男孩一起坐下，继续解释道：

"身体不知道我们真正是谁，"他说，"真相是，我们都是宇宙，我们选择来这个星球体验不同的经历，帮助我们学习和成长。我们自己选择我们的家庭和我们爱的人，我们选择要学习的功课，我们甚至选择要让谁来帮助我们学习这些功课。"

"作为宇宙，我们使用身体就好像使用交通工具一样，比如一个小汽车。我们的身体把我们带到这个星球的不同地方，这样我们就可以和在其他身体里的宇宙交流。"

他告诉男孩们，他们选择在这一生成为名叫盖博瑞和杰森的两兄弟，这样他们可以一起互相帮助，互相学习并成长。他还告诉他们没有死亡，因为宇宙从来不死。

"当一个身体失去了它的生命，"他继续说着，"只是表面上显得它已经死了。而真正发生的事情是，宇宙作为生命能量已经在这个身体里达到了最高限度的学习和成长，于是它就离开了这个身体，继续去选择其他的体验。这叫作'精神永存'。"

爸爸站起身来准备去工作了,最后他告诉男孩们:"如果你们一直记得你们是谁这个真相,还有你们为什么在这里,你们就会充满爱和喜悦地生活在一起。"

杰森和盖博瑞现在明白了。他们对彼此感觉到强烈的爱和喜悦,并继续讨论着爸爸的话,两人在内心深处都知道这是真相。

"你知道吗,盖博瑞,"杰森说道,"我不知道我们两个谁先完成'精神永存',如果你先,你得答应我一件事。你要承诺一直和我在一起,而且在我在这个身体的时间里都为我做指导。"

盖博瑞对弟弟微笑着说:"我答应你,而且你也要对我做同样的承诺。"

说完,两个小兄弟大笑起来,互相握手拥抱,并答应永远不忘记他们的承诺。

之后没几天,盖博瑞发生了一场看起来是悲剧的意外,并做了他的"精神永存"。

这对全家来说都是悲伤的时刻,而杰森特别难过。他感到巨大的空虚,因为他和哥哥盖博瑞特别亲近,而且他真正学会了将盖博瑞看作他的朋友、兄弟和老师。

杰森坐在他的房间里,悲伤地看着他和盖博瑞一起玩的玩具,他突然听到了一个声音。他向房间四周看了看,但是没有人。

然后他又听到了这个声音,这次是大声喊着:"我还在这儿!我没有离开你!"

杰森再次向四周看去,仍然没有看见任何人。他很好奇地问这个声音:"你是谁?有人躲在这里吗?"

这个声音回答道:"别害怕,是我,盖博瑞。我在遵守我的承诺。你只要聆听我,做我指导你的事情,我们两个都会很开心的。"

杰森还是看不到任何人,但是他可以非常清晰地听到盖博瑞的声音。杰森非常兴奋,他毕竟没有失去他的兄弟!

"我都等不及告诉爸爸妈妈你还和我在一起,"他说,"他们会高兴坏的!"

但盖博瑞迅速地回答:"不,你不能告诉我们的父母,因为你是唯一能听见我说话的人。我的承诺只对你,杰森。我和爸爸妈妈没有达成这样的协议。"

杰森再次尝试道:"但这真是太酷了,盖博瑞!我们应该告诉其他人!"

"不,杰森,"盖博瑞回答,"这只是在你和我之间。"

杰森安静地坐下,想着他的兄弟和这个协议。"你会在这里待多久?"他问。

"你想要我和你在一起多久我就待多久。"盖博瑞回答。

杰森下楼时,看见父母那么悲伤,他真想告诉他们盖博瑞还和他在一起,但是盖博瑞让他承诺不告诉任何人。杰森知道信守承诺很重要,他也知道盖博瑞相信他能做到。因此,他也相信盖博瑞,知道他的兄弟这样坚持一定有重要的原因。

杰森看到妈妈和爸爸默默哭泣时,他听见盖博瑞的声音说:"没事的,杰森,有一天我们会告诉他们的。谢谢你遵守了你的诺言。我们的语言非常有力量,因此对每个人来说,信守承诺都非常重要。"

于是故事就这样开始了⋯⋯

注 释

作者创作了盖博瑞和杰森,以便让读者更好地理解每个故事里呈现的内容。读者并不需要认识某个做了"精神永存"的人才能理解故事,并在他或她的日常生活里使用这些理念。

第一天·第一个故事
我观察我说了什么

第二天早晨,杰森很早就去学校了,这样他可以在课程开始之前打篮球。穿过操场时,他看见了他最好的朋友——汤姆。

"嘿,杰森,发生了什么事?"汤姆问道。

杰森忍着没哭,开始告诉汤姆他哥哥发生的悲惨意外。在故事讲到一半时,他听到盖博瑞的声音。

"杰森,停下!"盖博瑞说。

杰森假装弯下腰去系鞋带,以便可以听到他哥哥的声音。

"经历一次还不够难过吗?"盖博瑞问,"现在你知道我没有死,你还要再讲一遍这个故事吗?我仍然活着,和你

在一起，所以开心起来，开始玩吧！"

杰森系好鞋带，站起身，向他的朋友微笑着："忘记这个故事吧，汤姆。我们来这儿是玩的，让我们去投篮吧！"两个男孩互相击掌，跑向了篮球场。

正当他们玩篮球时，汤姆停了下来，看着杰森，说："我不敢相信你对你哥哥的事并不感到太难过。"

杰森发现自己又开始悲伤起来，而且又要重新走进那个故事和剧情时，他再次听见了盖博瑞的声音："坚持住，杰森。放下它，请放下它。你忘记了我就在这里和你在一起吗？请回到玩耍的喜悦中吧，并记住什么是真正正在发生的事情。"

杰森转向汤姆说道："嘿，我来这儿是要玩儿篮球的，这样我就暂时不用想那个了，你介意吗？"

汤姆举着手说："好吧，好吧，我再也不谈论那个啦。让我们玩球吧。"

两个好伙伴重新回到了欢乐时刻，一直投篮到上课铃声响起。

第二天·第二个故事

我留意我听到了什么

在后来的几天里,杰森发现,当学校里的其他孩子和老师们谈论他哥哥的"精神永存"时,他就会受到影响。没有人知道盖博瑞还活着。他们都相信他已经死了,因为他已经不在他的身体里了,所以他们就认为他死了。

一天，杰森离开教室，经过走廊时，碰到一个老师。老师叫住他并开始哭起来。

"哦，杰森，"她说，"对于你哥哥发生的事，我真难过。我知道你一定非常想念他，你一定非常难过。"

杰森听到老师说的话，觉得自己快要哭了。但这时他听见盖博瑞说："弟弟，这个老师不知道我和你在一起，但是你知道，你知道我在这里，所以不要仅仅因为其他人相信这些是真的，就相信他们告诉你的故事。"

杰森迅速将自己从悲伤情绪中拉回来。他微笑着感谢了老师之后，说他得回教室了。

当他跑到走廊上，记起关于他哥哥的真相，感到一股和平的感觉流经全身。他非常高兴自己没有因为别人不真实的信念而变得难过。

老师看着杰森离开，对这个男孩表情转变得如此迅速非常惊讶。有一刻他看起来快要哭了，然而马上一个大大的微笑点亮了他的脸庞，然后他就非常欢快地跑了。

那天傍晚，杰森回家的路上问盖博瑞："我还要听别人的废话多久呢？"

盖博瑞解释道："你越少关注别人不真实的信念，他们就越快停止和你谈论这些。就只是简单地放下他们的话，杰森。"

第三天·第三个故事
我觉察我看到了什么

一天中午，杰森到食堂吃午饭，看到两个同学因为家庭作业正在无意识地争吵，并且互相推推搡搡。他眼睛紧紧盯着他们，几乎都离不开这个争斗的场景了，而且当他看着这一幕时，感觉到巨大的混乱。

突然间，他感到有人碰他的肩膀。他转过身来，却并没有人。

"是你吗，盖博瑞？"他问。他听不见盖博瑞的声音，但作为回应，他感到肩膀再次被碰触了一下。他哥哥似乎正试图把他从争斗的场景中拉开。

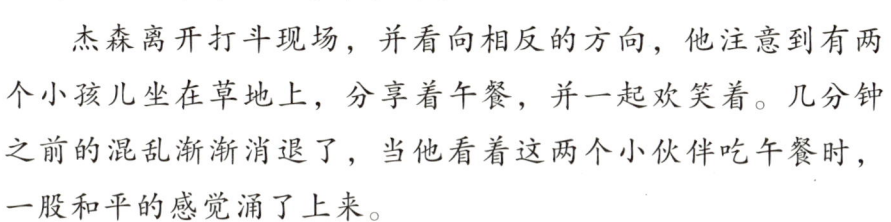

杰森离开打斗现场，并看向相反的方向，他注意到有两个小孩儿坐在草地上，分享着午餐，并一起欢笑着。几分钟之前的混乱渐渐消退了，当他看着这两个小伙伴吃午餐时，一股和平的感觉涌了上来。

然后，杰森开始再次听见盖博瑞的声音。开始是微弱的，随后愈来愈响亮，越来越清晰。

"哦，盖博瑞，"他说，"我真高兴又能听到你的声音了！我知道你和我在一起，但是我刚才听不到你的声音了。"

"当你处于沮丧或是混乱中时，你就被情绪控制着，所以就听不到我的声音了。"盖博瑞回答，"对你来说非常重要的是，觉察你正在看什么。当你看使你沮丧的情景时，混乱就将阻挡住我的声音和指引。你有没有发现，当你开始看那两个小伙伴欢乐地吃午餐时，你是多么迅速地又能听到我的声音了？"

"是的，你是对的。"杰森说，"一旦我看一些和平喜悦的事情，而不是看充满混乱的东西时，我就又可以听到你的声音了！从现在开始，我要一直警醒于我在看什么。我将从带给我混乱的情境中撤离，并将只看带给我喜悦和平的事情。"

第四天·第四个故事
我并不知道我所看见的真正意义

一天晚上，杰森做了个噩梦，他尖叫着醒来，睁开眼睛时，看见一个男人的影子躲在门旁边。

他非常害怕，紧紧闭着眼睛，希望男人认为他还在睡觉，然后就会离开。当他再次睁开眼睛偷看时，看见男人的影子在房间里迅速移动着。

杰森正要喊妈妈或爸爸进来救他，这时他记起一件重要的事情。"盖博瑞总是和我在一起的！"他想道，"我要在我的脑子里呼唤他！"

就在他呼唤盖博瑞的那一刻，他听见一个温柔的声音回答："怎么了，我亲爱的弟弟？你为什么叫我呢？"

"哦,盖博瑞,"他耳语道,"有个可怕的男人在我房间里,而且他准备攻击我!请帮帮我!"

"杰森,没有人在你的房间里,除了我们。"盖博瑞说。

"哦,但是有别人在这里,"杰森低声说,"我可以看见他!我可以看见他!"

"我亲爱的弟弟,"盖博瑞用慰藉的口吻说,"你睡衣的帽子上有根绳子垂下来,挂在你眼前。这就是你看到的怪物。"

杰森慢慢将手伸到眼前,轻轻地触碰挂在那儿的绳子,意识到盖博瑞的话是真的,如释重负地喘了一口气。

盖博瑞继续用充满爱的语调说:"你做了个噩梦,我的兄弟,你用恐惧给一根无害的绳子赋予了怪物的力量。你在这儿看见的并没有任何真实的意义。一条绳子怎么能是怪物呢?只是你赋予它的含义使它对你来说是个怪物。你赋予它的含义和现实没有任何关系。现在,你还害怕吗?"

杰森重新安睡在枕头上,说:"不,盖博瑞,我不再害怕了。"

"很好,"盖博瑞回答,"一旦你看见真相,就意识到你是安全的,没有东西要伤害你。我想要你记住一件非常重要的事情。你所认为你看见的并不总是真相。问问我你看见的含义,我会告诉你。"

杰森听到这些非常兴奋:"也就是说我不用再揣测一样东西的意义,只要问你就好了?而你会告诉我它的真实含义。我不会对我看见的东西再犯这样吓人的错误了?"

"是的,我的兄弟。"盖博瑞说,"让我告诉你每样东西的真实含义,而你再也不会害怕了!"

杰森大笑着说:"好的,成交!"

第五天·第五个故事

我愿意看见光

几天以后，杰森有一个考试。他很紧张，因为他觉得他学习得还不够，不能得到好成绩，但是他知道他能得到哥哥的帮助。

"盖博瑞！"他快速地说，"在教室里看看谁有正确答案。

你一发现答案，就马上告诉我！好吗？"

"你必须看向你的内在，杰森，"盖博瑞回答，"正确答案就在那儿。你必须放下关于你不够好，不知道正确答案的担忧。你已经尽力学习了，只要敞开你的头脑接收正确答案，它们会来的。"

杰森还是没法放松。他太焦虑了！"哦，求你了，盖博瑞。"他请求道，"你就到处找找看，看看那些最聪明的小孩的卷子，给我找到正确答案行吗？"

"如果我那样做了，杰森，你会认为答案是来自你之外的，而你将不会明白它们已经在你之内了。你只需要放松，然后允许你的头脑思考。让它敞开向它所知道的，这样答案就会来的。"

杰森看出来他没办法说服盖博瑞给他答案，而且他也知道盖博瑞以前总是给他正确的指引，于是他决定信任他。过了一会儿，他不再感到担忧，他感觉好像被一个柔软的和平宁静的毛毯包裹起来了。

杰森自信地微笑着，开始看试卷上的问题，相信所有正确的答案都在他自己的头脑里，就像他充满爱的哥哥告诉他的一样。当他读着每一道题，答案轻松地来到他的头脑里，他就把它们写了下来。

"谢谢你，盖博瑞。"他每写下一个答案就会这样自言自语，"谢谢你提醒我答案全部在我自己的头脑里。"第二天，当杰森看见试卷上的优秀成绩时，更加喜悦了。

第六天·第六个故事
我警醒于光

第二天早晨,杰森走进厨房吃早餐时,听见父母正在讨论爸爸的工作。

"我觉得我要被炒鱿鱼了。"爸爸忧心忡忡地说道,"我恐怕在工作中做得不够好,老板对我不满意。"

杰森的妈妈很安静,但是也显得很担忧。

这时,杰森听见盖博瑞说:"杰森,你要帮助爸爸改变他的思想,把光与和平带进他的头脑。"

"改变他的思想?"杰森问,"这是什么意思?"

"如果他继续持有这些黑暗的思想,他真的会被解雇。"盖博瑞解释道,"但这不是因为他的老板不喜欢他,而是因为我们的思想是如此强大有力,无论我们相信什么,什么就会呈现。"

"好的,盖博瑞。"杰森说,"我会尽我所能。"他走向爸爸说道:"爸爸,我知道你很担心被解雇,但是你可不可以试着改变你对这个事情的想法呢?"

父母惊讶地互相看了一眼。"改变我的想法?这是什么意思,杰森?"爸爸问道。

杰森解释道:"有人曾经告诉过我,我们的思想如此强大有力,无论我们相信会发生什么,很快就会真实发生。因此如果你改变你的想法,开始想你工作得很出色,你的老板很欣赏你,你将会看到他真的欣赏你。然后你想工作多久就能工作多久了。"

爸爸妈妈再次互相看了看,很惊讶他们的儿子说出如此成熟的话。爸爸拉过杰森,让他坐在膝盖上。"你成长得这么快,儿子!他们在学校教你们这些东西吗?"

在杰森回答之前,妈妈说道:"他是对的,亲爱的!他说得有道理。如果你改变对于这种状况的态度,我们都会感觉更好。"

爸爸认真想了想儿子的话,还有妻子刚刚说的。最后他同意了。"是的。"他说,"你们都是对的。我会改变我的态度。最起码,我不用这么担心。"

因此,从那天起,爸爸确保自己所想的是,工作非常出色老板很喜欢他,而且他的老板真的很欣赏他。没过多久,老板为了表示有多么赏识爸爸,给他加了薪水。

第七天·第七个故事
我非常富足

这件事第一次发生的时候,杰森正在教室里等着午餐铃声响起。他心里起劲地想着一个他想要的电脑新游戏,这时盖博瑞突然问他这个游戏要多少钱。杰森告诉他,需要三十五美元。

"如果那是你渴望的，那么你就会得到它。"盖博瑞说，"只要跟随我。"

杰森很困惑："跟随你是什么意思？"他问，"我都看不见你，怎么跟随你呢？"

"我的意思是，去我指引你去的地方。"盖博瑞说，"这样到今天结束的时候，你就会有足够的钱买你的游戏了。"

"真的？"杰森不相信地问道。他一开始很怀疑，但他已经领略到盖博瑞告诉他的事总是会变成真的。慢慢地，他开始对这个说法越来越兴奋。最后他说："好吧，盖博瑞，请你指引我，我会跟随你的。"

午餐铃响的时候，盖博瑞说："你吃饭前去厕所洗个手怎么样？"

"这是个好主意。"杰森说。他走进男生厕所，走向水池。

"水池下面是什么？"盖博瑞问道。

杰森低头向下看了看，看见角落里有张皱巴巴的五美元纸币。他把它捡起来，抹平，瞪着它。"这是开玩笑吧？"他咯咯笑着，"你的意思是就是这么容易？"

盖博瑞为他兄弟的喜悦而高兴。"是的！"他解释道，"就是这么容易！"

杰森跑去食堂，和最好的伙伴吃了午餐，又在午餐时间结束前去玩儿了一会儿篮球。在投篮和来回运球几分钟后，

杰森投了个特别高的球，球越过篮板落到操场边的栅栏旁边了，他跑过去捡球。

"杰森，栅栏上面飘动着的是什么？"盖博瑞问。

杰森侧身去捡球，注意到一张绿颜色的纸卡在栅栏里，在微风中拍打着。他靠得更近些一看，欢喜地跳了起来，这是一张十美元的纸币！现在他已经有了十五美元了！

放学后，他一蹦一跳地向家走去，感觉非常非常富足。知道无论何时他需要钱，在盖博瑞的帮助下他都会立即得到它，这真是太美妙了！

就在他离家还有几个街区的时候，他经过了一个男人，这个男人的年纪和他爷爷差不多。男人站在院子里，对着一棵树在说话。杰森很好奇，于是又靠近了一些。男人继续和树说着话,杰森听见他说:"过来,布多,爬下来,到爸爸这儿来,爸爸给你准备了好吃的,布多。"

杰森靠得更近些朝树上看去,男人转过身来说:"嗨,小伙子,我猜你大概奇怪我在做什么,是吧?"

"嗯,有点。"杰森说。

男人指着树说:"我的布多,哦,就是我的猫,这个世界上我最心爱的猫就在那儿。它被一只巨大的德国牧羊犬追到那棵树上了!"

杰森透过树枝看见了那只猫。"这不是很高,"他说,"它跳不下来吗?"

"我想它可以,但是它太害怕了。"男人说。

杰森以前在自家院子里爬过树,于是说:"我打赌我可以把它接下来给你。"

男人眼睛里闪烁着希望的光芒,说道:"你真的觉得可以吗?"

"是,我爬树可棒了。"杰森边说边把背包放在草地上。

他抓住一根树枝攀爬到树上,只用了两分钟。他抓起布多,将它裹进T恤里,然后爬下树,安全地回到了地面上。杰森将猫咪递给它的主人时,男人的眼睛里充满了欢喜的泪水。

"哦,我真不知道该如何感谢你。"他说,"布多是我在这个世界上的全部。"

"哦,别在意,这对我来说很容易。"杰森说道。

杰森弯腰拾起背包,准备回家了。男人伸手拿出他的钱包,取出一张二十美元的纸币。

"请拿这些钱给自己买点好玩的吧!"他说。

杰森愣在那里,瞪着钱。

男人大笑起来："请拿着这些钱吧，孩子。我真的想要你拿着！"

杰森咧嘴笑着，大声地说了声："谢谢你！"然后接过二十美元，一路向家跑去。

那天晚饭时，他告诉了爸爸妈妈当天发生的所有事情，还有他收到的刚好够他买游戏的钱。他没有提到盖博瑞的帮助，但是他告诉了父母他所学到的。

"无论我想要什么，如果我真的想要，它总会以某种方式提供给我。我所要做的就是希望某样东西，然后放下这个愿望，接下来奇迹就发生了！"

杰森的爸爸和妈妈注意到他脸上闪烁着喜悦和自信的光芒，他们清晰地感觉到了他是如此富足。

第八天·第八个故事

每个人都希望为我贡献

杰森感觉非常富足！一段时间以来，无论他想要什么，都会轻松地出现在他的生活里。就好像他有了自己的愿望精灵！

杰森知道他不再需要去渴求，担忧或是疑虑，他感到无限自由，他一直生活在喜悦和欢笑中。

没过多久，每个人都想要接近杰森。就好像他身上有股魔力，每当别人靠近他，他们就会感受到无忧无虑的快乐，就像杰森感受到的一模一样。

人们以各种方式为杰森奉献，他们给他各种礼物。在学校里，他的同学们给他玩具、游戏，还有额外的午餐点心。他的老师们经常给他的功课提供帮助，各个运动队的队长都想要选他加入他们的运动队。

在家里，妈妈做他最爱吃的饭菜，而且无论何时只要他要求，都会带他去购物，爸爸则经常带他到公园去打篮球，这是他最爱做的事情之一。

杰森感到被爱包围着。他不断感谢盖博瑞，还有其他给他东西、提供帮助的人们。

一天下午，杰森从学校回家时，他问盖博瑞："为什么每个人都一直想要给我东西？"

"哦，也许因为你是个好人，而每个人都知道这个。"盖博瑞说。

杰森默默地走了一会儿，想着盖博瑞的话。最后他问："你不认为他们是因为你离开身体了而同情我吧？"

"不，一点儿也不。"盖博瑞回答，"他们想要给你东西，首先是因为你感谢一切，而其次，你总是这样快乐和喜悦。使得每个人都想为你做些什么。"

杰森微笑着说道："我想我开始明白了。"

第九天 · 第九个故事
我值得富足

就这样奇迹不断地过了一个多星期，杰森又开始担心了。他仍然没有完全明白为什么每个人都贡献这么多给他。他怀疑他是否真的值得拥有这些礼物，是否值得人们一直给他提供帮助。

盖博瑞立刻来回应杰森，他向杰森保证他真的值得所有人这样做。随后盖博瑞告诉他为什么。

"亲爱的杰森，"盖博瑞说，"你是如此精彩的人！你总是欢笑，你心中充满爱和喜悦，人们情不自禁地爱你！"

杰森想了想说："哦，我猜这是真的。我注意到当我来到某个心情不好的人身边时，这个人会突然振作起来，并开始和我一起欢笑。"

"就是这样！"盖博瑞说，"人们在你身边时，会感觉到在他们的内心拥有和你同样的喜悦和爱——这就是你给他们的礼物，因此他们也把喜悦和爱回赠给你。有时候，喜悦和爱可以是一个微笑，有时候是话语，有时可能是你想要的帮助，还有的时候是礼物，它们全都是贡献给你的完美的东西。现在你完全明白你为什么值得每个人贡献给你美好的东西了吧？"

杰森嘟哝着："哦，我也许明白了。"

盖博瑞飞快地说："这远比'也许'要多得多，杰森。你绝对是值得的！而且非常重要的是，你要一直提醒自己你值得拥有所有精彩的东西。你记得我们谈论过你的思想有多么强大吧？"

"我记得。"杰森说。

"好吧，你不想形成自己不值得拥有精彩事物的想法吧？"盖博瑞说道。

杰森认真思考了一会儿。盖博瑞是在告诉他，如果他开始相信他不值得拥有美好的东西，那么他就再也收不到美好的东西了。

他让这一点深深地印在脑海里，直到他彻底理解。"你是完全正确的。"他告诉盖博瑞，"我是一个精彩的人，我值得拥有所有来到我身边的精彩事物，我们值得拥有来到我们身边的一切美好的事物！"

带着这个认知，杰森决定不再怀疑，他的人生中是否值得所有人都为他奉献。

第十天·第十个故事
我敞开接受宇宙所有的礼物

接下来的一个星期里,一天,杰森正准备离开教室时,他的同班同学布兰妮手里拿着一个小盒子走向他,她把盒子递给他说:"杰森,我有一件礼物给你。"

这是本周以来同学第三次送他礼物了,杰森已经习惯接受了。他接过盒子，微笑着感谢布兰妮。

杰森看着手里的盒子，开始觉得有点儿不舒服。他记得盖博瑞的话："你值得拥有"。他真的明白他确实值得拥有来到他生命中的所有精彩的东西，但是现在他有些困惑。

盖博瑞知道这时杰森在想什么。当他的兄弟需要他的时候，他总是在这儿。"怎么了，杰森？"他问。

"又一件礼物。"杰森安静地说。

"我注意到了。"盖博瑞回答，"这不是很棒吗？"

"哦，是的。"杰森说，"对我来说是很棒，而且我知道我值得拥有，但是盖博瑞，那其他人呢？为什么我这样特别？为什么不是每个人都值得拥有精彩的东西呢？"

"我的兄弟，"盖博瑞说，"其他人也都值得拥有精彩的一切！"

"那为什么不是所有人都能随时拥有精彩的东西，就像一直发生在我身上的这样？"杰森问，"我甚至什么都没做，它们就发生了！"

"你什么都不用做，只要敞开接受。"盖博瑞解释道，"对所有人来说，非常重要的一点是知道他们值得拥有精彩的一切，并且敞开去接受这一切。大多数人都没有敞开接受，因此他们也就没有接收到。就是这么简单。"

杰森似乎很迷惑，于是盖博瑞进一步解释着："这就好像在一个关着门的房间里，门外是一个奇妙世界，在那里你可以得到各种礼物，得到所有你能够想到的喜悦和爱，还有所有你能想到的快乐体验。敞开接受就好像是打开门，简单地迈出步子，进入那个仙境。"

杰森认真地听着，于是盖博瑞继续说："当你没有敞开接受的时候，就好像站在关闭的门前而不开门。另外一边是所有奇妙美好的东西，而如果你不打开门，你就不能享受到。当所有人像你一样敞开接受时，他们就会像你一样接收到。"

"对每个人来说，真的就是这样容易。"杰森说，"没有人需要做什么，只是敞开接受就足够了。"

盖博瑞很高兴弟弟听懂了，他欣喜地回答道："你完全正确！而这也正是你能听到我说话的原因，杰森。如果你不是敞开接受我的指引，我'精神永存'之后，就不能和你这样交流了。"

杰森很高兴他能敞开接受，因为这样可以让他和哥哥交流。他永远感谢这个奇迹。

第十一天·第十一个故事
我给予等同我接受

第二天,杰森看着房间里收到的礼物,他想着自己的生活变得多么轻松啊,现在每个人总是给他提供帮助,并为他做事。

他看了看四周,惊叹道:"我要拿这些礼物做什么呢?"随后他悄悄喊道,"盖博瑞,你在吗?"

"我在这儿,我的兄弟。"盖博瑞回答道,"有什么需

要帮忙的吗？"

"哦。"杰森说，"我糊涂了。我非常感谢收到这些精彩的礼物，但是我不可能全都用上，有这么多呢！"

盖博瑞温柔地回答道："是时候让你学习给予他人了，杰森。"

"给予他人？这是什么意思呢？"

"对你很重要的一点是，你要像接受一样给予。"盖博瑞说，"如果你抓住每样东西并把它留给自己，那么绝大部分的东西就留在那里未被使用，而你甚至都不知道你还拥有它们。留下你要用的，把其余的送出去。这样做了，你会记起你有这么多精彩的东西。"

"但这些是我的东西。"杰森打断说，"它们是我的！我怎么能把它们给别人呢？"

"正是因为它们是你的东西，你才可以把它们送出去。"盖博瑞解释道，"当你收到某样东西时，它就已经是你的了，但当你把它送出去的时候你才知道你真正拥有它。你肯定不能送出你没有的东西。"

"好吧，我明白物质的礼物是这样的。"杰森说，"但如果不是一个像玩具或是游戏那样的礼物，而是对我的一个好意呢？就好像人们在学校里帮助我，或为我做饭，或是带我去好玩的地方。我可以把这些善意也当成礼物送出去吗？"

"绝对可以！"盖博瑞大声说。他很高兴弟弟迅速理解了给予不仅仅包括物体。"善意是收到的最棒的礼物，也是可以给予的最棒的礼物。在收到和给予善意的过程中，你的心充满了爱。"

杰森非常兴奋！现在他都等不及要体会给出一些他收到

的精彩礼物会是什么样的感觉。盖博瑞告诉他看看周围谁会需要一些喜悦和欢笑，于是他将背包装满礼物，决定在这天结束前全部送出去。

他将第一件礼物给了妈妈，她坐在餐桌前，看上去有点忧郁。杰森进门时将手伸进背包，拿出一个同学送他的毛茸茸的泰迪熊。

"妈妈，我爱你！"他说，"我想送给你一个泰迪熊，因为你是这么完美。"

妈妈的脸顿时被点亮了，她接过泰迪熊，拥抱了儿子，看着他跑出去。

在上学路上，他经过一栋房子，门前草地上坐着一个大约五岁的小男孩。"你妈妈呢？泰乐。"杰森喊着。

小男孩回答："她去拿点心了，就来。"

杰森蹲下来问道："你干吗呢？"

泰乐说："我在试着系鞋带，但是总也系不上。我想给妈咪一个惊喜。"

杰森问："你能给我看看你是怎么系的吗？"

"好。"泰乐说。

杰森看着小男孩系鞋带，他注意到有一个地方泰乐做错了。"我想应该这样。"他说。然后他温柔地拿起小男孩的手，引导他做正确的动作，"你这样绕个圈。"

"哦。"泰乐说。

"现在，你自己试试另一只吧。"杰森建议道。

泰乐认真地跟着杰森的动作，成功地系好了另一只鞋带。"我系好了！我自己系的！"他开心地尖叫起来。

杰森微笑着站起身，这时他听见泰乐的妈妈从屋子里走出来。

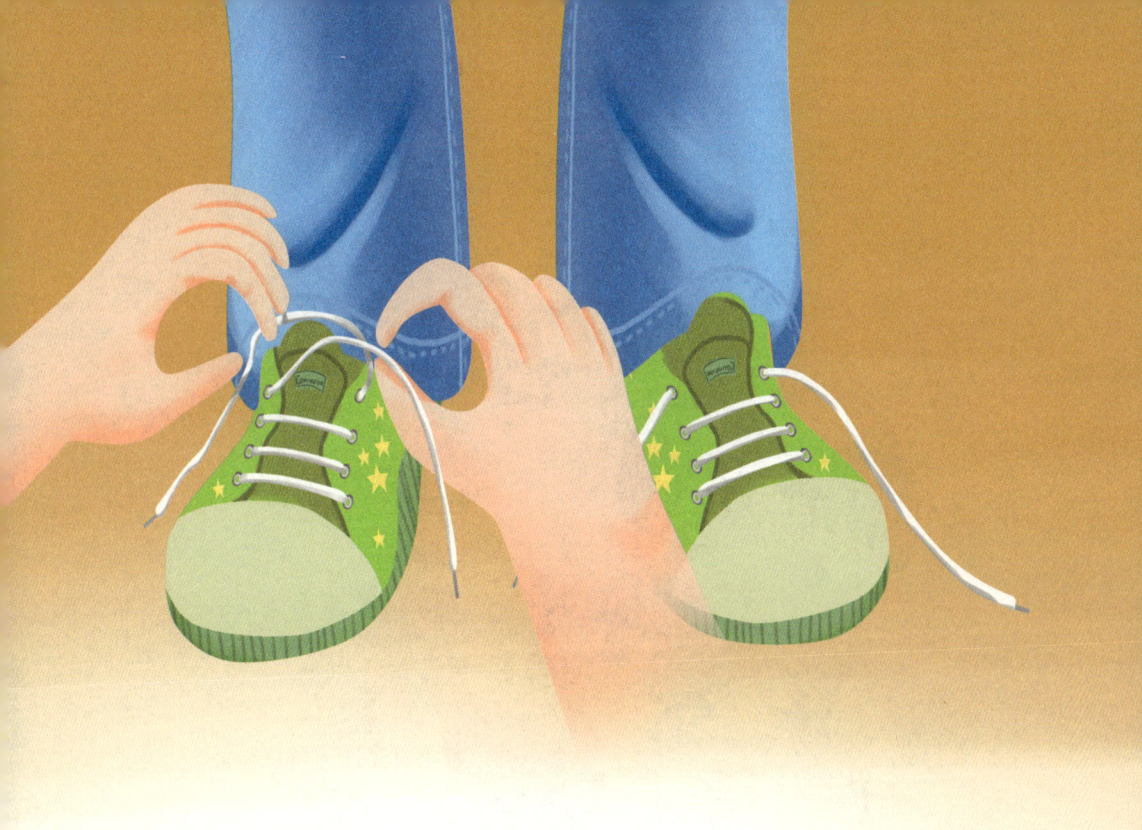

"泰乐，"她喊道，"你还好吗？"

泰乐跳起来跑向房子，大声喊着："妈咪！我做到了！我做到了！"进门前，他转回身喊道："谢谢你，杰森！"然后跑回房子里了。

杰森继续走向学校，他感到有股爱的暖流在心里流淌。当他记起盖博瑞告诉他的关于善意的礼物时，情不自禁地微笑起来。

在这一天结束的时候，杰森将随身带的礼物全部送了出去，背包里的，还有他心里的。晚上躺下睡觉时，想着所有送出去的礼物，内心深处涌起一种巨大的和平、喜悦和爱的感觉。就好像他漂浮在天空中高高的云端上，阳光温暖地照耀着他。

他感谢盖博瑞给他的永不停止的指导，他感谢这个奇迹。

第十二天·第十二个故事
我释放所有恐惧

学校里流传着一个关于杰森的故事，说他非常强大，有某种指引一直跟随着他。有些孩子对这一点非常兴奋，他们希望接近杰森，而另一些则不理解，他们都疏远他。因为他们经常看到他和某个他们看不见的人交谈，他们对待他的方式和对待别的孩子不一样，他们将他视为奇怪的或是疯狂的人。

过了一阵，杰森开始害怕别人对待他的方式。他跟他们在一起很困难，他试着想表现出他们认为正常的那样，然而这很不容易，因为他经常和盖博瑞交谈。

一天下午，杰森从学校回家，看见一些孩子在街对面盯着他，对他指指点点。他立刻变得害怕起来，脖子后面的汗毛都竖了起来。然后他听到了盖博瑞的声音："我的兄弟，你为什么这么害怕？"

"他们认为我是怪物。"杰森耳语道。

"不，我的兄弟，他们不认为你奇怪。"盖博瑞回答，"他们可能对待你和对待其他小孩不同，但这只是因为他们意识到你是多么强大，他们知道你在和某个他们看不见的人交流。"

"那么这个恐惧是哪里来的？"

盖博瑞解释道："你恐惧是因为你不明白为什么有些人待你不同，是你选择了这个恐惧的原因，所以你害怕。你相信那些人不喜欢你，但真相是他们非常喜欢你。他们只是不了解你。因为他们没有接触到他们内在的高级智慧，高级智慧会教导他们去理解，并因此带给他们和平

的感觉，这样他们对你的态度就会改变了。释放这个恐惧，我的兄弟，你的头脑里没有它的空间。"

杰森听着盖博瑞充满爱的声音，开始明白了，他考虑释放恐惧。他想象一片黑暗的云被排到了身体外面，然后以和平之光来填补。他觉得奏效了，一股和平的感觉开始涌上来包裹着他。

看到这儿，盖博瑞继续说："昂起头，知道你是多么强大。所有的人们迟早都会发现他们都有自己的高级智慧——无论是像我这样的一个充满爱的兄弟，还是其他为他们留在那儿的充满爱的天使，就像我为你留下一样。"

这时，杰森彻底处在和平之中了，他完全放下了几分钟之前掌控他的那份恐惧。"你是说每个人都有高级智慧？"

盖博瑞大笑着回答："是的，所有的人都有高级智慧，无论他们是否选择聆听，这取决于他们自己。而我非常高兴的是你选择聆听。"

第十三天 · 第十三个故事
我敞开心扉走向和平

一天,杰森从学校回到家,听见客厅里传来吵闹声。他的爸爸妈妈正在争吵,互相喊叫着。他靠近门廊,听到他们在争吵工作太辛苦,而钱又不够用。

杰森听到父母这样争吵很难过,他都快要哭了。他蹲下身子用手捂着脸，希望自己能做点什么，但他不知道能做什么。过了几分钟，他站起来，跑到楼上自己的房间里，关上门，扑到床上，开始抽泣。

抽泣中，他听见盖博瑞充满爱的声音。

"别哭，我的兄弟。"盖博瑞喃喃地说道。

"但你没有听见他们在楼下争吵吗？"杰森问，"他们争吵，互相指责，说没有足够的钱！"

盖博瑞轻声说道："没事的，我的兄弟。他们在经历他们自己的功课。爸爸不明白他拥有世界上所有他想要的钱，而只要他知道他有，他就可以让自己得到。"

杰森似乎有些困惑，于是盖博瑞继续说道：

"有些人认为只有通过辛苦工作，才值得拥有很多钱。还记得我们说过我们的思想是多么强大，我们所相信的必定实现吗？"

"我记得。"杰森说。

"也就是说，"盖博瑞说，"如果有人相信他们必须辛苦工作才能得到很多钱，那么除非他们非常辛苦地工作，否则他们不允许自己拥有想要的那么多钱。"

盖博瑞等着杰森思考了一会儿，继续解释道："妈妈也在做同样的事。"他说，"她感觉她在家里做的事情还不够多。因为这个，她就觉得自己不值得拥有她想要的东西。"

杰森还是想要为他们的争吵做点什么，于是问："那我能做些什么吗？"

"是的，杰森。"盖博瑞回答，"你知道我们的父母是多么棒。他们现在真的需要你的爱，因为他们已经没多少爱了。但是首先，你必须从自己的混乱中走出来，并向和平敞开你的头脑。当你将和平带给自己,你就能给他们带来和平。"

杰森从床上坐起来,擦干眼泪,深深地吸了几口气,试着想一些和平的东西。他的脑海里浮现出的画面是,一只鸟在空中自由翱翔,在鸟的下方,一股清泉慢慢流过岩石。杰森看着这个画面,并想着水流安静的声音,几分钟之前的混乱消失了。他感觉到了和平,并且清晰地知道该做什么。

他下楼来到客厅,父母看见他时,安静下来。他走向妈妈,给了她一个拥抱,说:"妈妈,你真棒!我刚刚注意到房间多么干净,并记得昨天的晚餐多么美味,而且我想告诉你我真的感激你。全世界再也没有比你更优秀的妈妈了!"

跟妈妈拥抱了很久。妈妈看着他,微笑着,突然感觉非常和平。

然后杰森给了爸爸一个大大的拥抱,说:"爸爸,你也是如此精彩!你总是给我每样我需要和想要的东西,而且你总是和我一起玩儿。我真高兴你是我爸爸,你值得拥有世界上每一样东西,因为你是全世界最棒的爸爸!"

爸爸的脸被喜悦点亮了,他说:"谢谢你,杰森!我真希望你早点进来。"然后,他看着仍然在儿子带来的和平里微笑的妻子说,"我们根本不知道在吵些什么,亲爱的,现在一切都很好。"

三个人拥抱在一起,温暖而甜蜜。

"好吧,"妈妈最后说,"小伙子们,你们准备好开始另一顿美餐了吗?"

杰森和爸爸都喊道:"是的!"然后他们三个一起走向了厨房。

第十四天·第十四个故事
我认出我的最佳利益

杰森的班级要开展一个科学活动。他的老师,琼斯太太,要求学生们分组工作,一个男生搭配一个女生。琼斯太太要求男孩们在教室的一边排成一队,女孩们在教室的另一边排成一队,这样他们可以更容易地结成对。杰森将自己精确地排在队伍里,确保自己可以和苏西配成对,苏西是他很喜欢的一个女孩。

当琼斯太太开始给学生们分组时,两个从图书馆回来的男孩走进教室,琼斯太太快速地把他们安排到队伍最前面。杰森简直不敢相信自己的眼睛!他都要崩溃了,因为他不再站在和苏西配对的位置上了。

当他感觉混乱正在体内升腾时，听见盖博瑞说："没事的，杰森。冷静下来，琼斯太太这样做是对你最好的。"

杰森并没有被逗笑，他将一只手放在嘴上，假装打哈欠，对盖博瑞耳语着："你是什么意思？'对我最好的'？和苏西结对才是对我最好的。"

"耐心一点，我的兄弟。"盖博瑞说，"你的天使知道什么会带给你最大的和平和喜悦。"

杰森知道盖博瑞总是对的，所以他能做什么呢？尽管一开始很不容易，他还是开始慢慢放下想要和苏西配对的想法。他悲伤地看着她被配对给尼克，他们穿过教室，去开始他们的活动了。

他数了一下女生队，看看谁会是他的搭档。当意识到是阿西莉时，他再一次不敢相信自己的眼睛。他和阿西莉上周刚吵过架，并且杰森决定永远都不再和她说话了。

很快，他和阿西莉都走到了队伍最前面，他慢吞吞地走过去和她成为搭档。阿西莉则带着失望的表情跟他一起穿过了教室。

他们坐下来整理项目材料时，杰森试着想一些话和阿西莉说，但是他非常不舒服，什么都说不出来。

这时盖博瑞说："你不是真的想要继续和阿西莉生气吧？看看这带给你的混乱吧。告诉她你很抱歉，杰森，你上周伤害了她的感情。"

杰森不想搭理盖博瑞。上周阿西莉说他和不存在的人说话，像个疯子，这引发了他们之间的争吵，所以他只是等着。他不再和阿西莉或是盖博瑞说话，只是静静地按照琼斯太太的要求整理活动材料。

他再一次听见盖博瑞的声音:"说吧,杰森,向阿西莉道歉,这样做不会有任何损害,事实上,如果你这样做了,你会感觉更好的。"

杰森还是忍着,几分钟没说话。

再后来,他意识到他哥哥是对的,他转向阿西莉说:"阿西莉,我对我说过的话道歉,很抱歉我叫你胖大妈,我真的不是这个意思。"

阿西莉抬起头看着杰森,她的眼睛吃惊地瞪圆了。"真的?"她问。

"真的。"杰森边说边咧嘴笑着。

看到杰森咧嘴大笑的样子,阿西莉也忍不住笑了:"知道吗,杰森?我并不是真的认为你和看不见的人说话就是发疯,实际上我认为你非常有智慧,因为你做的每一件事都非常棒。我真的很尊敬你,你是一个出色的伙伴。"

杰森顿时感觉到那股熟悉的、温暖的和平和喜悦感包围了他。他以前就一直喜欢阿西莉,甚至比喜欢苏西更甚,但是他从没想过自己可以和她做朋友,他一直认为阿西莉是个势利眼。但是现在,他第一次看到她是一个温柔、充满爱的人。他紧紧地握住了她的手。

阿西莉的眼睛闪烁着特别喜悦的光芒。"我就知道你会成为我的搭档,尽管我们那时候不排在一起。"她说。

杰森大笑着问:"你怎么知道的?"

"我就是知道。"她回答,也紧握了一下他的手。

两个新朋友一起开始他们的活动时,杰森抬头看了看琼斯太太,悄悄地感谢天使通过她安排了他的最佳利益。

第十五天·第十五个故事
我有耐心

圣诞节过几天就到了,这是所有人的欢乐时光,大家互相交换礼物,都感到开心喜悦。

杰森家的圣诞树下,有一个大大的盒子写着杰森的名字,他都等不及要打开那个盒子了!每个清晨,每个夜晚,他都

看着那个盒子，猜想里面是什么。他希望可以打开他，但是父母说他必须等到圣诞节那天才能打开。

他乞求爸爸妈妈让他早点打开，但是没用。他们告诉他要有耐心，而且他们很坚持这个决定。他必须等待。

终于，圣诞节的早晨到了。许多亲戚都过来交换礼物。甚至贝蒂奶奶都从澳大利亚赶到这里，和家人们一起过圣诞节。

贝蒂奶奶带来许多礼物，杰森看见其中有一个小小的包装很漂亮的盒子，上面写着他的名字。

拆礼物的时间终于到来了，杰森抓过他看了好几个星期的大盒子，撕开包装纸。打开盒子时，里面的东西让他脸上绽放了一个大大的笑容。那是一个遥控机器人！他几个月前在商店里看见时就希望能得到。

"谢谢妈妈！谢谢爸爸！"杰森一边大叫着，一边在盒子里找电池给机器人装上。

杰森把盒子翻过来把里面的东西全都倒出来，没有找到电池。他在盒子周围找了找，也没有电池。他真想立刻就玩机器人，但是既然没有电池不能玩儿，他就开始拆别的礼物。

杰森继续打开礼物，他兴奋地发现有这么多好东西——好看的衣服，新游戏和书，还有很多好玩的玩具，其中有些也需要电池。但是，那些礼物也都没有配备。

杰森继续拆着礼物，他拿起贝蒂奶奶那天早晨带来的礼物，拆开一看。"哇噢！"他欢呼着，"谢谢，贝蒂奶奶，这就是我需要的！电池！"他现在有了机器人和其他玩具需要的所有电池，而且有富余呢。

杰森开心地大笑着，贝蒂奶奶轻声笑着解释道："我知道那些为你买需要电池玩具的人们会忘记配电池，所以我的任务就是提供它们。"

杰森跳起来给了奶奶一个大大的拥抱。他意识到耐心等到圣诞节早晨再拆礼物真是做对了，如果他早一点儿打开，就会失望地发现这么好玩儿的玩具因为没有电池而玩儿不了。

因为他很有耐心，所以避免了失望，取而代之的是他和家人一起愉快地享受了这个精彩的圣诞节。

第十六天·第十六个故事
做出反应前,我暂停片刻

这是一个美丽的晴天,午餐时刻到了。杰森和好朋友汤姆坐在操场的草地上吃午餐,他们正吃着三明治,另一个班级的男孩瑞澈走过来说:"嗨,杰森,你是个非常酷的家伙。"

杰森看了看瑞澈,微笑着说:"谢谢。"

瑞澈在杰森身边坐下,他们聊了一会儿学校里的事,汤姆静静地坐在旁边听着。

"知道吗,杰森?"瑞澈说,"我父母出城了,我哥要

在家里办一个派对,他告诉我可以请一些我的很酷的朋友。你想要来吗?"

杰森咯咯笑着正准备接受这个邀请,突然听到盖博瑞的声音说:"在你回应之前暂停一会儿,我的兄弟,首先看看那是个什么样的派对。"

杰森暂停了一下,问道:"那是个什么样的派对?"

"哦,你知道的。"瑞澈回答,"就是给'潮人'准备的。我哥哥有很多很酷的朋友,他们会给我们酒和烟,或许还有些别的什么。我们会玩得很HIGH(开心)的!"

杰森震惊了:"你们要做那些不该做的事情?"

瑞澈轻声笑着说:"好吧,还有别的什么是'潮人'会做的?这就是为什么我们酷,不是吗?"

杰森安静下来,他记起父母总是告诫他不要沾染烟和酒。他知道过量的烟和酒精损害大脑和身体,而那些酗酒和嗜烟的人毁掉了他们的人生，过得非常不开心。

他已经准备好对瑞澈说些非常尖刻的话，但是他听到了盖博瑞的声音。

"杰森，不要生气。"盖博瑞说，"瑞澈会以某种方式学习到他的功课，你的任务就是为你自己做正确的决定。你不需要和他一起玩或是接受他的邀请，不要让他的行为影响到你。"

杰森明白了。"谢谢你的邀请，但是我没有兴趣参加这样的派对，那不是酷的表现。"他对瑞澈说。

这时候，杰森和汤姆吃完了午餐，他们站起来，和瑞澈道别，走回教室。当杰森和瑞澈交谈时，汤姆一句话都没有说，而这时，汤姆脸上浮现出大大的笑容，看着杰森，用手肘轻轻碰碰他，说："哇噢！你处理得真棒！你真的是最酷的！"

杰森大笑着回答："是啊，这很容易！"然后他悄悄感谢了盖博瑞的指引。

盖博瑞回应道："我的兄弟，只要我和你在一起，你就不会陷入麻烦，因为我总是指引你通往和平的方向。谢谢你敞开接受我的指引，我爱你。"

杰森悄悄地回答："我也爱你。"

第十七天·第十七个故事
我敞开接受奇迹

很快就到学期末了,杰森在准备期末考试。尽管花了很多时间学习,他还是担心考试结果。他很想门门都得优,但又认为这不可能,因为有些功课实在是太难了。

杰森花很多时间想着考试,很久都没有和盖博瑞交谈,甚至是想起他了。一天晚上,他正在房间里学习时,突然感

到一阵无助和失控感，他开始哭起来，直到累得哭不动为止。他筋疲力尽，安静地躺在床上，闭上眼睛，试着和平。

"我好久没想到盖博瑞了，"他突然意识到，"我想念他。"

好像是在回应他的想法，盖博瑞说："是时候了，我的兄弟！我以为你忘记我了！"

"盖博瑞！"杰森回答道，"你去哪儿了？我好久没有听到你的声音了！"

"我就在这儿，但是你都没有想起我。"盖博瑞说，"你忙着担忧你的考试。知道吗，杰森，无论何时只要你担心，你就关上了和我沟通的门，我没法进来和你说话，因为你听不到我，你听到的都是你的担忧。"

杰森静静地躺在那儿，过了一会儿，盖博瑞的声音带来了他寻求的和平。

"你现在能听见我的声音是因为当你哭的时候，清理了头脑里所有的焦虑，并意识到你希望能处于和平中。"盖博瑞补充道，"这敞开了你的头脑，这样你就能接受我的帮助了。"

尽管现在杰森冷静下来了，他仍然想着他的考试。"我担忧我的期末考试成绩，而且我并不知道该做什么。"他说。

"我亲爱的兄弟，你所能做的就是停止担忧！"盖博瑞回答，"担忧恰恰是你烦恼的根源。"

"但如果不担忧，我怎么能确保努力学习并都得优呢？"杰森问。

盖博瑞说："这很简单，你只需要信任你的高级智慧。记住，你的身体并不是你，你和宇宙合一的那个部分才是真正的你！当你信任你的高级智慧，你的头脑就把学习这件事敞开向喜悦和平，并敞开自己接受奇迹，就是门门都得优。当你敞开接受奇迹并且知道你值得拥有它们时，它们就会呈现出来。奇迹总是在那儿，就只是等着你的接受。"

杰森想了一下盖博瑞说的话，他不明白是什么让他如此担忧，但是他知道他不想再担忧和混乱了。

他非常高兴盖博瑞提醒他，他不只是个无助的身体，他知道自己要宏大得多！他以前见识过他头脑创造的力量，他决定立刻就信任他的高级智慧，并敞开接受所有等着他接受的奇迹，他知道自己值得拥有它们。

现在杰森感到非常和平，他觉得这天已经学够了，决定明天再以清醒的头脑继续学习。他钻进被子里，用充满爱的声音和盖博瑞道了声晚安后，很快进入了深沉的梦乡。

几天之后，考试全部结束，成绩也出来了，杰森并不惊讶每门课都得了优。他感到非常高兴，爸爸妈妈也非常开心。

他知道他值得得全优，并且知道只要他敞开接受奇迹，所有精彩的东西都会向他呈现。

第十八天·第十八个故事
我只选择和平

一天下午,杰森从学校回家时,发现父母正在忙着用气球和彩条装饰房子。

杰森走向爸爸,拥抱了他一下说:"嗨,爸爸,干吗呢?"

爸爸搂着杰森说:"今天是我和你妈妈的结婚纪念日,我们邀请了一些亲朋好友过来一起庆祝,这将会是一个美妙的夜晚!"

"太棒了！"杰森说，"我的堂兄弟们也会过来吗？"

爸爸咧开嘴笑着回答："当然！"

"好嘞！"杰森喊道，"我得把我的电脑设置好，准备些游戏一起玩！"

当他跑向卧室时，爸爸在后面喊他："杰森，等一下！"

杰森停下来转过身："怎么啦，爸爸？"

"你今晚有作业吗，儿子？"

杰森迅速地回答："不，没有。"

爸爸笑着说："那好吧，去准备好玩儿的吧！"

杰森上楼到他的房间时，他的胃感觉非常难受。他对爸爸说谎了，他晚上是有作业的。

他爬楼梯时听见盖博瑞说："杰森！你为什么说谎？"

杰森很尴尬，不知该如何回答。对爸爸说谎已经很不爽了，更糟的是现在盖博瑞也知道了。

为了回应杰森的想法，盖博瑞说："我是你的一部分，我的兄弟！我知道你的每一件事情。"

杰森到了房间，关上门，悄悄回答："我不知道为什么要说谎，我就是不想马上就操心我的作业。"

盖博瑞温柔地告诉弟弟："杰森，你知道学校的作业是非常重要的，如果作业没做完，你就会整晚都担心它，而且也不可能玩好。"

"不，我不会的。"杰森迅速回答，然后他垂着头坐在床上，"我会，我会很好的。"他站起身走到书桌边开始设置他的电脑。

盖博瑞想要和杰森说说缘由。"弟弟，"他轻声说，"当你内心深处处于混乱的时候，不可能玩得开心。你必须选择和平，只有和平，只有通过选择和平，你才能经历喜悦、快乐和欢笑。别想把喜悦和开心建立在混乱和担忧之上，那是行不通的。"

杰森坐在电脑前，想着盖博瑞的话。这些话非常有道理，而且他知道这是对的。他当然想要和平，但是一想到今晚的派对，他就不想做作业。

杰森想着应该怎么做时，盖博瑞继续道："还有，兄弟，记住我们是谁。我们的话语非常强大，我们必须只说真相。当你向爸爸说谎，告诉他你没有作业要做的时候，你忘记了这一点，而现在你就觉得不舒服了。说谎违背你的本性，在内心深处，你知道这一点。"

这时，杰森听见爸爸叫他下楼，盖博瑞的声音渐渐变小了。他走到客厅，知道他必须纠正，他必须告诉爸爸真相。

"嗯，爸爸。"他开了个头。

但是爸爸打断他："哦，杰森，谢谢你下来。我真高兴你什么作业都没有，我们真的要你帮忙！在你装游戏之前，先帮我和你妈妈把这些装饰弄完好吗？"

杰森听到了盖博瑞温和的声音："真相，我的兄弟。要说真相，你不需要说谎。"

此刻盖博瑞的支持给了杰森莫大的力量，他看着爸爸的眼睛说："爸爸，我有些事告诉你。"

爸爸弯下腰，看着杰森说："什么，杰森？"

杰森开始说："我很抱歉，爸爸，我对你说谎了，我今晚有作业，很多，而且我想在派对开始之前做完，这样我才能感到和平，并且真正玩得开心。"

爸爸安静地看着杰森，看了好一会儿。

杰森不确定爸爸要做什么，但无论是什么，他都已准备好接受。

妈妈默默站在那儿,也不知道会发生些什么。

突然间,爸爸微笑着抱住了他:"哦,杰森,你太了不起了!我真的爱你!感谢你告诉我真相,真希望你哥哥能在这儿,看见这些他会为你骄傲的!"

杰森微笑着喃喃地说:"比骄傲还要多。"

妈妈看着形势转变,松了一口气。她也拥抱着杰森,在他耳边轻声说:"你真是个不可思议的孩子!"

接下来杰森花了两个小时完成了家庭作业。做完时,他感觉轻松自由并且非常和平。然后他跑下楼,刚好赶上迎接他的堂兄弟们。他们整晚一起玩游戏,开心极了,而且杰森完全没有想起他的功课——一次也没有。

那天晚上杰森躺下睡觉时,盖博瑞问他:"今晚你感觉如何,我的兄弟?"

杰森充满和平地微笑着说:"有你在这儿,我真是太幸运了!每件事都很精彩,我今晚玩儿得开心极了,如果没有你我不可能做到,谢谢你盖博瑞,我爱你!"

那晚杰森睡着之前,他听见盖博瑞柔和的声音说的最后一句话是:"我也爱你。"

第十九天·第十九个故事
我充满爱，值得被爱

一个星期六的晚上，杰森的两个朋友——汤姆和吉姆，来他家过夜。男孩儿们在一起听音乐，讲笑话，一起大笑，开心极了。吉姆玩儿得有点疯狂，一个晚上踢了三次便携式CD机，还划坏了杰森的CD唱片。

杰森有点儿生气了,他转向他的朋友说:"吉姆,别再碰 CD 机了,你今天晚上已经毁了三张 CD 了!请不要再碰 CD 机。"

吉姆低下了头,走到房间的另一边,脸上带着受伤的表情。

汤姆和杰森互相看了看,耸了耸肩。然后杰森把 CD 机和其他一些重要的游戏机从地板移到台子上,以防被损坏。

过了几分钟,男孩子们都忘了这个意外事件,又一起开心地玩起来。

第二天早晨,吉姆和汤姆的父母来接他们回家。汤姆说了再见,并感谢杰森让他在他家过夜。"周一学校见!"他边喊边跑到街上,向在车里等他的妈妈挥着手。

吉姆的爸爸在汤姆走后很快就来了。吉姆听见外面门廊传来喇叭的嘟嘟声时,打开前门,转向杰森说:"我再也不到你家过夜了,你太小气了。你都不让你的朋友玩你的游戏机还有其他东西!"不等杰森回答,吉姆就跑向爸爸,叫着,"嗨,爸爸!"

杰森惊呆了,觉得很受伤。尽管他认为吉姆的说法并不真实,但还是有一股羞愧和自责感向他袭来。毕竟,他希望朋友们来他家玩得开心。

杰森关上前门,听见爸爸在厨房叫他:"早饭好了!过来吃吧,杰森!"

他感觉胃里有点恶心,头也在痛,想起食物就要吐。他走进厨房说:"爸爸,我现在还不饿。"知道爸爸会坚持让他吃早饭,他迅速补充,"我等会儿再吃,好吗?"

爸爸关切地看着他,弯下腰摸着杰森的额头说:"你的脸看上去很苍白,伙计。你觉得怎么样?"

"没事。"杰森说,"我有点胃痛,我想躺一会儿。"

爸爸拥抱了一下杰森说:"好的,伙计。如果我能做些什么,告诉我。"

"谢谢,爸爸。"杰森边说边转身走回房间。

杰森走上楼梯,感觉不太好,对于可能会失去吉姆这个朋友,他感到很难过。他走进自己的房间,轻轻关上门。

门一关上,隐隐约约地听见他哥哥盖博瑞的声音。他知道那是盖博瑞,但是听上去那样遥远,他听不真切盖博瑞在说什么。杰森知道是他头脑里的混乱阻止他听见,而他要冷静下来,让和平进入他的头脑。他躺在床上,深深地呼吸,每一次呼吸,他都释放掉羞愧、内疚和悲伤的想法,并用光和爱充满他的整个头脑和身体。

这个做法奏效了,杰森开始感到和平流向自己,而他可以清楚地听到盖博瑞关切的声音了。

"杰森,怎么了?你为什么沮丧?"

"我感觉很糟,因为我对吉姆很吝啬。"

"我的兄弟,你不吝啬。"盖博瑞静静地说,"吉姆有破坏游戏机和玩具的习惯,而你很爱护玩具。你叫他尊重你的东西完全没有错,你做了正确的事情。"

"但是我感觉很差。"杰森回答,"我喜欢他,而他告诉我他不想再来我家了,因为我不让他玩我的东西。"

"没事的。他会改变主意的。"盖博瑞向杰森保证,"你忘了你是一个充满爱的人了吗?你爱每一个人!而你也被大家所爱,每个人都爱你,因为你善良而温柔。"

"但是,"盖博瑞接着说,"不要为别人的习惯和问题买单。如果吉姆喜欢破坏东西而你不让他破坏,那是他的问题,你不需要有任何内疚。对于你，非常重要的是，总是对自己诚实，并做对你来说正确的选择。"

杰森觉得盖博瑞的话有道理，他开始对自己感觉好起来，他很高兴要求吉姆尊重他的东西。但他仍然关心一件事，并问盖博瑞："你确定吉姆会回来吗？"

盖博瑞温柔地问："我曾经错误地引导过你吗？"

杰森大笑着说："不，盖博瑞，从来没有。"

现在，杰森的头不痛了，肚子却开始饿得咕咕叫了。他下楼到了厨房，父母还在吃早餐，他们看见杰森，放下了手里的叉子。

妈妈从椅子上站起来走向他。"你感觉怎么样，亲爱的？"她问。

杰森看着她说："好多了，妈妈。我现在需要的是成堆的馅饼和你们俩的拥抱。"

杰森用手臂环绕着妈妈，爸爸也从椅子上站起来，走向妻子和儿子，加入了他们的拥抱。他们互相表达了满满的爱之后，杰森欢呼道："开吃！"

第二十天·第二十个故事
只有爱存在，恐惧是幻象

一个没有月亮的晚上，杰森从学校走回家。他放学后留下来看了一部特别的电影，然而看完电影他也没有马上回家，而是留下来和一些伙伴聊天，现在他只好摸黑回家了。

杰森家和学校之间的道路旁边有一个棒球场，现在他正

穿过这个棒球场，今晚没有棒球比赛，灯都关着，四周非常黑，他很害怕。

突然，杰森听见有沙沙的响声好像从儿童区旁边的灌木丛里传出来。他不由自主地想起从其他小孩那儿听来的故事，无家可归的人在黑夜里游荡，到处偷东西，还有心术不正的人绑架小孩，并且伤害他们。这些想法吓坏了他，他开始快步走起来。

他似乎听见身后有脚步声，更害怕了。他迅速转身，但是没看到有人。

他现在走得更快了，而且瞥见一棵树后面似乎藏着一个身影。

他正要尖叫逃走时，记起盖博瑞对他说过很多次："只有爱是真的，杰森，别的都不存在。恐惧和产生恐惧的原因都不是真的，那只是幻象，所以不要听信于它。"

"不要相信它。"这句话语浮现在脑海里，这给了他莫大的勇气。

那一刻，杰森停下脚步，站在人行道上，非常冷静地回过身来，望向尽头的黑暗。然后他大声对自己说："我不害怕，没有什么好怕的，我相信这只是个恐惧的幻象。"

杰森看看四周，意识到没有人跟着他，而他听见的脚步声也是他自己的脚击打地面传来的回声。现在他明白自己听到的灌木丛中的沙沙声是微风吹过的声音，而此刻微风正温柔地穿过他的头发。

他也意识到树后那个身影不是别的，正是树的影子在街灯的映照下舞蹈。杰森默默站着，闭上眼睛，感觉到和平和安宁笼罩着他。

突然，盖博瑞的声音像回声一样在他的脑海里响起："杰森！你终于能听见我了！我真高兴你放下了恐惧。在这里没有别人，除了你和我，还有一个无家可归的人，他在那边的树下平静地安睡着。"

杰森忍不住笑了。几分钟之前还让他害怕的念头现在看起来很荒谬。"哇噢，"他说，"是我自己精心营造了这一切，是吧？"

盖博瑞回答说："重要的是你将自己如此迅速地带出恐惧，

几乎和你进入恐惧一样快。干得好,我的兄弟!"

杰森微笑了,盖博瑞总是知道如何给他带来欢笑。

盖博瑞继续说:"现在有个人需要你的帮助,杰森。你往回走会看到你的同学杰妮,她也在沿着这条路回家。不幸的是,杰妮还没有明白恐惧是不存在的,她现在非常害怕,就像你之前一样,而她真的需要你的支持。"

这时,杰森心里充满了爱与和平,他毫不犹豫地走回去找杰妮。他知道恐惧可以给一个人的头脑带来多大的混乱,而他真的不希望杰妮有那样的感觉——一秒钟也不要。

他朝学校跑回去,一分钟后,就看见了杰妮。她快速地走着,每走两步就向两边瞥一下。他减慢速度靠近她。

"嗨，杰妮！怎么样？"

她的脸似乎被恐惧冻结了："杰森，我太害怕了。我猜想有人跟着我。"

杰森先是微笑，接着大笑起来："我了解，几分钟之前当我穿过这里时，我和你想的一样，直到我意识到真的没有恐惧。"

杰妮走慢了一些，有朋友在这儿，她显然安心了许多。"没有恐惧？"她问"这是什么意思，杰森？"

杰森继续说："我们通过想可怕的东西，把恐惧放进了自己的头脑。恐惧是我们自己制造出来的！其实恐惧根本不存在，杰妮。"

"但真的好像有人跟着我！"她回答。

"我知道，"杰森说，"但是转过身看一下，你看见人了吗？"

杰妮转过身，街道很安静，他们是这里仅有的两个人。她看向杰森，微笑着说："是的，我想没有。"

他们一起大笑了一阵，这时杰妮意识到了杰森说的是真相。随后她问："杰森，你介意和我一起走回家吗？"

杰森看了看她，突然觉得自己非常勇敢而且成长极其迅速。"当然不介意，我很愿意。来吧，咱们走吧。"

两个朋友一边走一边欢笑着，在那个没有月亮的暗夜里，杰森充满感恩地知道他再也不会恐惧了。

第二十一天·第二十一个故事
父亲无条件地爱着我

这是美丽的一天,杰森一家在公园里,妈妈在野餐区准备午餐,杰森和爸爸在湖里钓鱼。他们已经坐在岸边钓了一个多小时,但是一无所获。

爸爸转向杰森开玩笑地说:"要不就是湖里根本没鱼,要不就是我们是很差劲的渔夫!"

他们俩都大笑起来,杰森回答说:"爸爸,我想我们需要帮助。"

爸爸轻声笑着回答:"你说得对,什么帮助我们都要。"

但杰森是认真的。"我很快回来。"他说着慢慢从岸边退到附近的一棵树旁。

"你去哪？"爸爸喊道。

"等我一分钟，爸爸。"杰森回答。他坐在树下，悄悄呼唤盖博瑞。

"是的，我亲爱的兄弟。"盖博瑞回应着，"你有什么需要？"

"盖博瑞，"杰森开始说，"我真的想要捉一些鱼。"

盖博瑞大笑着："但是为什么呢？"

杰森认为答案很明显，就回答："因为这很有趣呀！"

"你要吃抓的鱼吗？"盖博瑞问。

杰森考虑了一下，说："哦，不，不是真的要吃，我就想要捉鱼。"

"好吧，所以你只是想要捉它们。"盖博瑞说，"那么你捉住它们之后要做什么呢？"

"哦。"杰森回答，"我想我会把他们扔回湖里。"

盖博瑞很高兴听到这个回答："如果是那样的话，看到你右边大约一百英尺（1英尺=0.3048米）的地方有一棵枝条低垂的柳树了吗？"

"是的，盖博瑞，我看见了。"杰森回答。

"好吧，就在那棵树附近的湖床上有个洞，里面有三条饥饿的大鱼正在找吃的。有两条正准备产卵，所以很重要的是你要放掉它们，你保证放掉它们吗？"盖博瑞问杰森。

"当然。"杰森回答。然后跑回岸边，爸爸正在那儿等着。

"快点，爸爸，跟着我！"他说着拉起爸爸的手走向盖博瑞告诉他的有鱼的地方。

爸爸非常惊讶，因为这是他第一次见到杰森做主。看见儿子表现得像个男人，他感觉很好。他跟随着杰森问道："我们这是去哪？"

杰森说："我知道有个地方有些鱼正等着被捉。"

爸爸感到很好笑，并且很好奇，所以就跟着走了。他们走近柳树时，杰森告诉爸爸柳树附近的湖床上有个洞。

"听起来不错。"爸爸说。

爸爸和杰森放下了鱼线，垂钓了几秒钟，就有鱼来咬杰森的钩了！

杰森开始回绕鱼线收杆，可是鱼太重了，线都拉不动了。

爸爸迅速把他的鱼竿用力插在沙子里，跑到杰森身边。他站在杰森身后，一只手握住鱼竿，另一只手帮助杰森拉线。

"我想你钓了条大鱼！"爸爸喊道。

"别让它跑掉，爸爸！"杰森兴奋地尖叫着。

他们激动的声音响彻了整个公园，妈妈也跑过来看发生了什么。接下来的十分钟，妈妈为丈夫和儿子鼓掌加油，最后他们终于钓上了这条鱼，这是他们见过的最大的欧洲鲈鱼！

杰森放下鱼竿，一家人看着他们的战利品在岸上扑腾着，爸爸喊道："真是个了不起的收获！我们把它洗洗，当今天的晚餐！"

"听起来不错。"妈妈说，她走回野餐区继续准备午餐。

杰森正准备同意，突然记起了他对盖博瑞的承诺。"不，爸爸，我们不能这样做。"他说，"我们得把这条鱼放回去。"

爸爸看着儿子，脸上的笑容消失了："你说什么呢，把它放回去？这可是我们美味的晚餐呀！"

"但是，爸爸，"杰森继续道，"我保证过要把它放回去。"

"保证？"爸爸疑惑地问道。

杰森不知道该如何回答："我现在没法儿解释，爸爸，但是我跟你说，这条鱼必须放回去。"

爸爸看出了儿子脸上急切的表情，他是认真的。"那好吧，这是你钓的鱼。如果你想放了它，我们就放了它。"

杰森松了一口气。"太棒了！"他喊着，然后弯腰帮爸爸轻柔地将鱼松钩。

爸爸看着儿子把鱼轻轻地扔回湖里，摇了摇头。"杰森，"他开始说，"我问你，如果我们的目的是要把鱼扔回湖里的，那么我们为什么一开始还要钓呢？"

杰森想了一下，"哦，爸爸，这其实不关钓鱼的事，我感兴趣的是和你在一起。"

爸爸有点蒙了，他把手放在儿子的肩膀上，看着儿子的眼睛说："什么？你说什么？"

杰森重复了一遍："这只是关于和你在一起，爸爸，我热爱我们一起做好玩的事，这不正是我们钓鱼的原因吗？我们在一起很开心。"

那一刻，爸爸感受到对儿子深深的、无条件的爱。他用手臂环绕着杰森，他们拥抱了很长时间。突然爸爸退后了一步，看着杰森，低语道："我们再去抓更多的鱼！"

爸爸的鱼竿还插在沙子里没动，就和他放下时一样。他收回线，发现还是没有咬钩，鱼饵都没被碰过。他帮杰森重新投了线，自己也重投了线，没多久，就感到了鱼竿被拉扯着。"咬钩了，杰森，我钓到了一条！"他边喊边收线。

杰森放下鱼竿，兴奋地跑到爸爸身边。他看着另一条大鱼被钓了上来，不像杰森钓的那条那么巨大，但也足够大了。他们看着鱼在沙地上跳了一会儿，然后互相看了看。

爸爸咧嘴笑着说："我们把它扔回去怎么样？"

杰森也咧嘴笑了笑："耶，爸爸！我能给它松钩吗？"

"当然。"爸爸回答，然后看着儿子轻柔地松开鱼钩，就像他早先做的那样。

杰森把鱼钩安全地从鱼嘴中取出，把鱼递给爸爸说："这次你放。"

爸爸接过鲈鱼，把它轻轻地扔回水里。

突然传来妈妈的喊声："午餐好了！过来吧，伙计们！"

杰森看看爸爸，说："哦，太好了，我饿了！我们吃完饭可以继续钓鱼吗？"

"当然。"爸爸回答，然后和儿子一起走回去，妈妈已

经准备好了一顿美味的午餐，有三明治，沙拉和水果。

狼吞虎咽地吃完了妈妈准备的健康食物后，杰森站起身说："谢谢，妈妈。太好吃了。"然后他转向爸爸问，"你准备好再去钓鱼了吗？"

爸爸刚好吃完最后一口苹果，说："我好了，老兄！"他站起来走向妻子，亲吻了她，说："谢谢，亲爱的，这顿午餐太棒了。咱们一起去湖边怎么样？我们的儿子是个钓鱼高手。"

杰森的妈妈愉快地加入他们，当她和家人一起走向湖边时，感觉到暖暖的爱围绕着她。

盖博瑞告诉杰森湖的另一边鱼非常多，因此在这一天里，好几十条鱼被他们钓了又放，放了又钓的。这是他们人生中最棒的钓鱼日。

回家的时间到了，他们三个收拾起所有的食物和渔具，走向车子。杰森感到强烈的爱流淌出来，他对父母说："我真的热爱这样的家庭出游，我们四个一整天在一起，玩得这么开心！"

妈妈咯咯笑着说："你说'我们四个'是什么意思？你的口袋里有只小老鼠吗？"

杰森大笑着回答："哦，我是说我们三个。"

他的父母微笑着看看对方，耸了耸肩。

到了车跟前时，杰森听见盖博瑞说："小心点，我的兄弟，你差点露馅！"

杰森咧嘴笑了笑，他感谢哥哥的指导，感谢围绕在他身边无条件的爱。

第二十二天·第二十二个故事
父亲爱我比我爱自己更多

一天,学校有一个特别的教师会议,所以很早就放学了。杰森沿着他往常的路线回家时,盖博瑞问他:"杰森,你今天想做些不一样的事吗,找点好玩儿的?"

杰森回答:"当然。有什么好玩儿的?"

盖博瑞建议:"今天咱们绕路回家,反正时间也很充裕。"

杰森也觉得改变一下,选择不同的路回家会很有趣。他

转过身，向绕远的那条街道走去。

杰森快到街角要转弯时，盖博瑞让他停下来。

"听我说，杰森。"盖博瑞说道，"到达街角时，你会看见一个大人正在怂恿你的朋友杰克去做坏事，别紧张，就保持很酷的样子走过去和杰克在一起。他很希望现在能有个朋友和他在一起。"

杰森犹豫了一下说："但这听起来很危险，盖博瑞。"

"不危险。"盖博瑞回答，"如果你听我的并完全按照我说的去做，所有事都会搞定。"

杰森并不很确定他要做什么，但他知道有盖博瑞的帮助，他会做正确的事情。他很兴奋将要发生的一切，同时也感觉很安全。

杰森转过街角时，看见杰克斜靠在一棵树上，正和一个盖博瑞早先描述过的男人交谈着。

杰森呼唤出内在的力量，顿时感觉非常勇敢。他径直走向他的朋友说："嗨，杰克！发生什么事了？"

男人被杰森的突然到来

吓了一跳，向后退了一步。

杰克转向杰森，他一脸受惊吓的表情，眼角还噙着泪水。他说："哦，没什么，杰森，什么事都没有，别担心。"

男人轻声笑着，靠近杰克，把胳膊搭在他的肩上。"是啊。"他用严厉的口吻说，"照你朋友说的做，别担心。小孩，就走你的路吧。"

杰森一动不动。"在我弄明白发生了什么事之前，我哪儿也不去。"

男人慢慢地将手臂从杰克的肩膀上移开，走向杰森站立的地方，不怀好意瞪着杰森说："小孩，如果你知道什么对你好，你就会照我说的走你的路。"

那一刻，杰森感到恐惧开始慢慢涌上他的头脑。随后他记起盖博瑞和他在一起，哥哥和他在一起的念头取代了恐惧的念头时，就听到盖博瑞说："保持冷静，我的兄弟，他伤害不了你，我在这里。"

这给了杰森继续下去的力量。他向男人靠近了一步，深深地看着他的眼睛："离开我的朋友，否则我就叫警察。"他用如此勇敢坚定的声音对男人说，以致他都有点认不出自己了。

男人惊呆了，他从未想过一个小孩会这么勇敢地面对他。他往后退去，眼睛里闪烁着疑惑，声音缓和了一点，说："小孩，这不关你的事，走开吧。"

"你错了，这关我的事，不和杰克一起走，我哪儿都不去。"他告诉男人。

男人顿时很生气，他抓住杰森的胳膊，但这时候的杰森感觉自己如此强壮，没有东西可以吓倒他。他继续听着盖博瑞说的话。

"杰森，现在我想让你完全重复我告诉你的话。"盖博瑞说。

杰森敞开头脑倾听并重复盖博瑞的话，他听见自己冷静地对男人说："听好，我知道你叫劳尔，住在景观村232号62室，你缓刑期的监察官是汤普森先生。"

男人被小男孩说的这些击中了，这个小男孩似乎知道他所有的事！

杰森可以感觉到男人抓他的手松动了，此时，杰森知道他成功了。

"你是想要我再多说一些，还是把你的手从我们俩身上拿开，然后赶紧离开？"他问男人，声音坚定而自信。

男人震惊地张着嘴巴，松开杰森的手臂，开始后退。他转过身指着杰克，咬牙切齿地说："你跟你的朋友离我远点，我不想再和你们说话。"

杰森和杰克看着男人转身，快速跑过街道转过街角，消失了。杰克松了一口气，转向杰森。

"哇噢！你是怎么知道他的事情的？"他说。

"别在意这个了，在他改变主意之前我们先离开这里吧。我要回家，你呢？"杰森回答。

"嗯、嗯。"杰克回答，他还没从刚才的震惊中恢复过来呢。

两个男孩子一起走回家时，杰森说："顺便问一下，杰克，你怎么和那种人来往？"

杰克垂着头，有点尴尬，小声说："我不会再和他说话了。你知道，杰森。"

杰克停顿了一会儿，感觉好像从肩膀上卸下了一副重担。

他看着杰森告诉他:"杰森,你刚才的表现是真正的好朋友,谢谢了,伙计。"

杰森朝杰克笑了笑说:"我想让你知道一件事,你有一部分是超越你身体的,这部分知道每件事,它连接我们彼此以及整个宇宙,这个高级智慧爱你超过你爱自己!正是这个宇宙之爱指引我走这条路,在你想要朋友的时候出现在你面前。"

杰克若有所思地望着杰森,当他听着杰森说的话时,和平的感觉涌上心头。某样东西——也许是他的高级智慧,告诉他杰森说的是真相。

杰森继续道:"如果你又试图把自己陷入那种场景里,请记起今天的经历,做更明智的选择。"

"我一定会的。"杰克大笑起来。

他们俩击掌约定从此以后要互相提醒多留意于此。随后他们继续走向回家的路,喜悦地感受着宇宙的爱环绕着两个人。

第二十三天·第二十三个故事
我信任我的父亲

夏天终于来了！一年当中，杰森最盼望这个季节，因为爸爸妈妈会在周末带他出去露营。他们决定这一年的首次露营去黄石国家公园。

杰森和父母在公园里徒步行走了一天，这是美丽的一天，

他们享受着原野，享受着它全部的美和它的无限生机。傍晚时分，他们来到露营地开始安营扎寨。

妈妈在准备晚餐，她让杰森去找一些木头来生火，晚饭后他们准备烤蘑菇。这是杰森最爱做的事之一，他高兴地走进树林，仔细挑拣，按照爸爸教的那样，只选好燃的木柴。

杰森走啊走啊，直到他找到足够生一堆火的木柴，才决定回露营地。他抬头看了看，突然发现不知该走哪条路了。他已经信步走了很远，现在迷路了。当恐惧开始抓住他时，他做了几个深呼吸来放松。对于如何不让恐惧掌控他的头脑，他现在已经掌握得很好了，所以他看了看四周安宁的景色，听了听大自然和平的声音，然后呼唤盖博瑞。

听到盖博瑞说："是的，我在这里，我们没有迷路！"杰森感到被巨大的和平感觉包围了。

他微笑着问："那为什么这里看起来一点都不熟悉？"

"你刚才翻过了一座小山，那座小山挡住了你的视线。"盖博瑞解释着，"如果你向右走，很快就会回去。"

杰森看向右边，注意到盖博瑞说的小山。他开始朝那儿走，突然，盖博瑞告诉他："等一下，杰森，别动，停在你现在的地方。"

杰森困惑地问："怎么了？我已经找到所需要的木柴，而且我饿了。"

"杰森，"盖博瑞温柔地继续说道，"我想要你站在那儿保持冷静，记住我和你在一起，而你可以信任我。"

杰森感觉到有些他没有觉察到的东西出现了。那种曾经的恐惧感开始蔓延，然而杰森提醒自己他信任盖博瑞，和他在一起绝对安全。

杰森听见身后的树林中传来沙沙声，盖博瑞冷静地告诉他："你后面有一头狼。如果你变得害怕并开始逃跑，狼就会追你，它觉得你在跟它玩。而如果你转过身看着它，欣赏它的美，它会感觉到你的镇静，也会保持镇定。"

杰森没有动，恐惧在召唤他。但是他信任盖博瑞，知道他说的是真的。于是他请求那个信任给他力量，让他做他必须做的事情。

盖博瑞很高兴杰森的冷静，他继续说道："现在到了你学习彻底信任的时候了，大自然创造这头狼出于完全的和平，只是你关于它恐惧的想法使它变得可怕而危险。"

深吸了一口气，转过身，映入杰森眼帘的是一幅美丽的

画面。他身后大约二十英尺的树林中站着一头灰色的狼，它的毛在夕阳映照下闪闪发光。当他的视线与狼接触时，杰森感到全身都起了鸡皮疙瘩，就好像整个森林的声音突然中止了。现在，一股极其巨大的和平和安宁笼罩着他们两个。

杰森以前从未见过活的狼。他慢慢坐在身旁的岩石上，低声惊叹道："你真美。"这种感觉极其真实，当杰森看着狼时，狼也盯着杰森，就好像它也正在欣赏杰森。

过了一会儿，狼开始朝杰森移动。杰森看着狼越来越靠近他，先前成功克服的恐惧又要淹没他时，他选择聆听盖博瑞的声音而不是恐惧。

"信任自然，我亲爱的兄弟。"他听见盖博瑞用充满爱的声音说，"这头狼来这儿不是要伤害你的。"

狼离得更近了，杰森呼唤着那份信任，他微笑着再次看向狼的眼睛。此刻和平在他们之间自由顺畅地流动着，就好像这两个生物之间彼此都感受到他们的连接。

杰森失去了时间感，他不知道他和狼一起在那儿待了多久。当他开始想到底过了多久的时候，狼优雅地走开，走进了树林。

狼离开了杰森的视线，杰森觉得兴奋替代了和平，他兴奋着刚刚所发生的事：他离一头活生生的狼只有几英尺！

杰森听到他哥哥欢快地说："热爱自然的感觉好吗？"

"哦，是的，好极了！"杰森说。

盖博瑞告诉他狼也是同样的感觉。"它感受到你的爱和信任，杰森，这就是为什么它能保持冷静。"

杰森抱着他收集到的木柴，回到了营地。他兴奋地告诉父母他碰见狼的事，爸爸显得有些担忧。

然而妈妈迅速地说："亲爱的，别担心了。杰森身上充满了爱，没有什么能伤害他，就好像有人在守护着他似的。"

爸爸不得不同意："哦，好像真的是这样，是吧？"

杰森微笑着，悄悄地喃喃自语："是的，盖博瑞在这里。"

父母认识到儿子被保护着，宽慰地大笑起来，当然，他们没有听到杰森的话。杰森也很宽慰，他知道他的父母也同样被保护着。

杰森将木头放入火坑，准备晚饭后烤蘑菇。那是他露营期间最喜欢做的事情之一，当然，更喜欢的是欣赏野生生命。

第二十四天·第二十四个故事
我父亲很伟大，我也是

半夜时分，杰森爬起来去喝水，这已经是他这晚第二次起来喝水了。杰森回到床上时，翻来覆去地折腾了好久就是无法入睡。

过了大约十分钟，杰森决定起来阅读。有时候他在睡前

阅读时，会困乏地睡着。也许现在阅读可以帮助他入睡。

他浏览着书架，想看看读哪本书，盖博瑞的声音进入了他的脑海。

"怎么了，我的兄弟？为什么你睡不着？"

杰森悄悄回答："我也不知道，盖博瑞。真的很奇怪。现在是半夜，但我很清醒。"

"你想谈谈吗？"盖博瑞问他。

过了一会儿，杰森回答："事实上，我是想谈谈。我有些问题问你。"

"好的。"盖博瑞愉快地说，"你在想什么？"盖博瑞很高兴能帮助杰森，他尤其喜欢教导杰森，让他知道他自己是多么强大和精彩。

"你死的时候发生了什么？"杰森开始说，"为什么你还能在这里，在我的头脑里和我在一起？"

盖博瑞咯咯笑着说："哦，这些就是半夜闯入你头脑的问题，怪不得你睡不着觉了。"

杰森可不想开玩笑，他只想要答案。"怎么啦？"他有点严肃地问道。

盖博瑞看出此刻杰森没心情开玩笑，他知道他得做点什么来照亮杰森。

"我会告诉你的，如果你真的想知道。"他温柔地对弟弟说。

"告诉我吧，盖博瑞。"杰森说，"我真的很想知道。"

"好吧。"盖博瑞说，"你记得去年我们和爸爸的谈话吗，他告诉我们来这儿是互相帮助的？"

杰森记得，就是这个谈话让他和盖博瑞更加亲密。

盖博瑞继续说:"就是那时爸爸告诉我们,我们永远不死,而他是对的。我们死亡时发生的事是,我们只是失去了对身体的知觉,转换成我们生命最初的形态——宇宙。作为宇宙,我们可以出现在任何时间、任何地点。而唯一限制我们的就是我们对身体的知觉。"

杰森虽然听懂了盖博瑞所说的话,但他还有很多困惑。他喜欢他的身体,而现在他不确定他是不是应该这样感觉。

他表达了他的困惑,盖博瑞告诉他:"我不是说你不应该喜欢你的身体,杰森。关键是你必须意识到你不仅仅是你的身体,你只是在身体里体验你自己,实际上你比一个身体大得多。"

当杰森开始明白这个真相时,他感觉非常强大。他的困惑消失了,这时盖博瑞继续说:"当你在你的真实状态里,也就是作为一个宇宙,你就能意识到你有力量创造每一件你希望的事情,并且有能力在任何时间去任何地方。我在这儿和你在一起是因为我选择这样,我们有协议的,记得吗?"

"我当然记得!"杰森微笑了,这是他人生中签订的最棒的协议!

他想起另外一个问题,就问盖博瑞:"你'精神永存'时痛苦吗?"

"不,"盖博瑞告诉他,"在身体显示死亡之前我就离开了身体。而且我想要你知道每一件你听说的关于疼痛和死亡的事情都不是真的。当你的时间到了,要做'精神永存'时,不需要感觉到任何疼痛,你真正需要做的就是让身体躺下,然后去任何你想要去的地方。"

"这对每个人来说都是真的吗?"杰森悄悄问道。其实

他在问的时候，已经知道答案了。

"是的，对每个人都是。"盖博瑞回答，"我们都是作为宇宙的一部分被创造出来，而且事实上，我们都和宇宙一样伟大。"

盖博瑞说话时，更多的问题闯入杰森的头脑。他问："如果我比我的身体要强大，为什么我不能在任何我想要的时候离开身体，却只能等时间到了才永远离开？"

"好问题！"盖博瑞喊道，"而答案是你可以，而且你做了！每天晚上当你的身体睡觉时，你的能量就离开去很多不同的地方，经历很多不同的事情。但绝大多数你醒来的时候，就不记得了。"

杰森对这个很兴奋："但是我有时记得，盖博瑞！有时候我醒来，记得和你在一起，而且似乎是在一些从未到过的地方一起玩得很开心。我总是想我只是在做梦，但有时又觉得不只是一个梦——它看起来太真实了。"

"它是真的，我的兄弟。"盖博瑞继续说，"我总是等着你出来和我一起玩，而我们确实玩得很开心。"

现在杰森觉得有点困了，躺在了床上，但在睡着前他还有一个问题。"盖博瑞，"他问，"你知道我什么时候'精神永存'吗？"

这是盖博瑞一直在等着的问题。他知道杰森最终会问的，而他也准备好了回答："是的，我知道，但这不确定。"

"什么意思？"杰森问。

"嗯，"盖博瑞继续道，"我可以进入未来，依照你现在的生活，你现在正在走的路看到你'精神永存'的时间，但如果你决定改变你生活的方向，你'精神永存'的时间也随之而变，这真的只取决于你。"

杰森知道这个答案很欣慰，他微笑着，睡眼蒙眬地说："你总是守护着我，是吧？"

盖博瑞体贴地回答："放心吧，我的兄弟，我一直和你在一起。"

杰森就要睡着时又问："我们今天晚上要出去玩吗？"

盖博瑞温柔地回答："我就在这儿等着你，杰森。待会儿见。"

第二十五天·第二十五个故事
我放手，让父亲指引我

又是一个美丽的周末，非常适合露营。这一次，杰森和父母去锡安国家公园度周末。搭好帐篷后，杰森和爸爸去河里漂流，也就是坐在轮胎里顺流而下，妈妈悠闲地坐在树荫下看书。

杰森和爸爸玩得很开心，一路大笑着顺流而下。突然爸爸注意到河的前方落差很大，水流急速下降。"跟着我！"他喊道，"这个好玩！"然后就消失在这个急流的边际，进入下方满是泡沫的水里了。

杰森很害怕，他迅速抓住附近的一根树枝，让自己停下来。

他向湍流的下方看去，想看到爸爸，但是哪儿都没有爸爸。

他紧紧抓住树枝，试图想出个办法，他觉得自己不可能冲下那个急流。

过了几分钟，他听见爸爸喊着："杰森！快来！"

杰森再次向河流下方望去，看见爸爸站在齐膝深的水里，左手抓着轮胎，右手正向他挥动着，让他下来。

"我在这里等你，快下来吧！"爸爸喊道。

杰森使劲抓住树枝。"不！"他摇着头喊道，"我害怕！"

"但是杰森，"爸爸再次喊道，"这个急流没有看起来那么深。不可怕，真的！"

杰森不愿放手，他只是不停摇头表示拒绝。

"杰森，"爸爸继续说，"你知道你是安全的！放下你的恐惧，信任你的高级智慧，他会照顾好你。你很安全，而且这很好玩！"

杰森试着放松，他深吸了几口气，闭上眼睛，听着水顺流而下的安宁的声音。

这时盖博瑞来了。"你还在等什么？我的兄弟。"他问。

杰森很高兴听到盖博瑞充满爱的声音。"这看起来真是个巨大的急流。"

"那只是因为你现在所在的地方看不见那边的底。"盖博瑞向他保证，"它真的不深，我都不害怕。"

杰森大笑起来："哈！你说说当然容易啦！你又不在身体里，而且你想去哪儿就去哪儿！但我还在我的身体里，而这个身体有时会受伤。"

盖博瑞咯咯笑着说："但是杰森，你在轮胎里很安全。爸爸说信任你的高级智慧是对的。你是来这儿玩的，只是你的想法让事情变得恐惧，放下那些念头，让你的高级智慧照顾你！你会很安全，而且会特别开心！"

杰森冷静下来，甚至他都没有意识到，他已经松开了树枝，漂向了急流。他闭上眼睛，但盖博瑞告诉他如果他一直睁着眼睛会更兴奋。

"这是个不可思议的急流，杰森。你不会想错过它的任何一部分。"

跟随着盖博瑞的指引，杰森就在被冲到边缘的那一刻睁开了眼睛。当他掉下去时，巨大的兴奋涌上来。

杰森抬起头，擦去溅入眼睛里的水，看见爸爸站在河边，正欣喜地鼓着掌。

"干得好！干得好！"爸爸喊道。他把他的轮胎扔进水里，立刻跳进河里去迎接杰森。

当他们碰头时，两个人的脸上都咧着大大的笑容。爸爸轻轻揉着杰森的湿发说："我真为你骄傲！看着你睁大眼睛，带着兴奋的笑容速降下来真是太棒了！"

"这真好玩，爸爸！"杰森喊道。

大约十分钟后，他们觉得玩儿够了，可以出水了，就互相帮着把轮胎推上岸。

走回营地时，他们一边大笑，一边谈论着激动人心的漂流和那个超级棒的急流。

快到的时候，杰森转向爸爸说："爸爸，当我们放下恐惧，信任高级智慧时，生活就变得如此喜悦，如此好玩，这是真的呀。"

爸爸看着杰森微笑着说："你明白这个了，伙计，不要忘记这一点！"

第二十六天·第二十六个故事
作为宇宙之子,我是有福的

为庆祝七月四日的美国国庆日,杰森的叔叔约翰要在家里举办一个小型派对。杰森真心喜欢约翰叔叔,他性格豪爽,开朗幽默,约翰叔叔的笑话总是让杰森大笑不已。他也非常慷慨,经常给杰森礼物,一件T恤衫,一个游戏,有时甚至是钱。

杰森一家很快就到了约翰叔叔家。杰森按了门铃,约翰叔叔满脸笑容地走出来迎接他们,他拥抱了哥哥、嫂嫂,然后举起杰森用力抱紧他,在他脸颊上亲了一下。

"哇噢!"约翰叔叔喊道,"你好像比我上次见你又长高了一英尺呢,老兄!"

约翰叔叔把他放到地上,杰森大笑着,擦了擦叔叔的口水。如果有什么对约翰叔叔不乐意的地方,那就是他大大的湿乎乎的充满口水的吻了。但约翰叔叔热爱这样亲吻别人。

约翰叔叔伸手从口袋拿出钱包。"我有样东西给你，伙计。"他跟杰森说，然后弯下腰来，递给侄子一张一百美元的纸币。

"一百块！"杰森喊道，"哇噢，谢谢你，约翰叔叔！"他用胳膊环绕着叔叔的脖子，给了他一个大大的拥抱，心里想着可以买好多炫酷的玩具了。

他松开手臂时，叔叔看着他说："杰森，我想让你知道，你是我最喜欢的侄子，我真心爱你，有你在我的生活里，我感觉备受祝福，因为你是这样出色的男孩。"

杰森感觉到叔叔无条件的爱包围着他。他转身看看他的父母，他们手牵手站在那儿，微笑地看着他，他意识到他有这样一个充满爱的家庭是多么有福。

前门突然被撞开，杰森的两个堂兄弟冲了出来，比赛着看谁先跟他打招呼。他微笑着，再次感觉到他充满爱的大家庭从他父母那一代延伸扩大开来，这真是太有福了。

美味的晚餐之后，约翰叔叔家有个烟花庆典，然后杰森和父母回家了。躺下睡觉时，他非常感谢有这样一个充满爱的家庭，他感到备受祝福。"盖博瑞，"他问，"每个人都能受到祝福，都有一个美满的家庭吗？"

盖博瑞告诉他："是的，但并不是每个人都能像你这样意识到这一点。如果你不知道你拥有一样东西，它就不能带给你任何真实的好处，就好像你根本没有它一样。"

"但是，"他继续说，"你总是意识到在你的生活中有着许多的祝福。你在哪里都能看到它们，由于你这样感恩，你就创造了更多祝福。"

"是你教我怎样做的，盖博瑞。"杰森睡眼蒙眬地回答，"你是我的祝福之一，而我也非常感激你。"他边说边慢慢进入了梦乡。

第二十七天 · 第二十七个故事
今天属于我的高级智慧

一个星期六的早晨,杰森醒过来,听见哥哥盖博瑞快乐地唱着歌:"早上好,阳光照,起床时候来到了!"

杰森嘟囔着翻了个身,拉过被子盖住脑袋。

盖博瑞继续说："快点，醒一醒，这是个美丽的早晨！"

杰森又抓过枕头捂住耳朵。

这让盖博瑞大笑起来："这些挡不住我，我的声音总是在你头脑里萦绕！"

杰森现在彻底醒过来了，他咧嘴笑着，掀开被子呼吸新鲜空气。

"你什么时候能再显现出来？"他问盖博瑞，"还是我永远只能听到你的声音而看不到你的样子？"

"目前，你还只能听到我，但时间到了，你也会看到我。"盖博瑞说。

杰森很高兴知道有一天会再次看到盖博瑞。

"那么，"他说道，"有什么事？你为什么在星期六这么早叫醒我？这可是我的懒觉日！"

"哦，今天会是非常特别的一天。"盖博瑞回答，"今天，我想让你在你的生活里放下控制，把那个控制交给我和你的高级智慧，并信任我们会带给你精彩的一天。"

杰森并没有真正明白盖博瑞的要求。他不认为他在试图控制他生活中的事，但是盖博瑞向他保证，即使我们没有意识到，我们也总是试图掌控。

"当我们把控制交给我们的高级智慧时，"盖博瑞告诉他，"我们总能经历宇宙为我们准备好的精彩旅程。"

杰森同意有意识地放下控制，而盖博瑞说会帮助他。

早餐之后，妈妈告诉杰森帮他预约了早上九点半理发，现在还有半个小时。杰森准备了一下，和妈妈准时到了理发店。

在前台查过预约后，杰森发现他的发型师格雷那天打电话说早上要晚一个小时来上班，所以只好换另一个发型师。

杰森和妈妈被领到大堂等待代班发型师。

几分钟之后,一个名叫茱丽叶的女发型师来到大堂告诉杰森由她来顶格雷的班。她示意杰森跟着她走,这样好给他洗头发。

对于一个女发型师给他剪头发,杰森感觉有些不舒服。他正准备抗议时,听到盖博瑞说:"你答应放下控制的。"杰森记起他们的约定,就决定让他的高级智慧来掌控整个局面。他站起身跟着茱丽叶来到水池边。

洗好后,杰森坐在茱丽叶指定的椅子上,她开始给他理发。他很爱理发,因为有人打理他的头发让他觉得特别放松。

他太放松了,竟然打了个盹,后来杰森听见吹风机的声音才醒过来。他揉了揉眼睛,看着镜子里茱丽叶正在吹他的头发。他注意到自己看起来非常不一样,茱丽叶把他的头发剪得比以前短得多。他惊呆了,瞪着镜子里自己不熟悉的影像。

大约五分钟之后,茱丽叶放下吹风机,拿开围在他脖子上的塑料衣垫说:"好了,运动员。"

杰森离开镜子,看了看旁边正等着他的妈妈。"哇噢!多帅的男孩!你觉得怎么样?"她问。

"妈妈,"杰森倒吸了口气说,"她把我的头发全剪了!"

妈妈回答说:"哦,是短了很多,但是亲爱的,看起来真的很好看。我喜欢这样!"

杰森正准备对茱丽叶说点难听的话时,再次听到盖博瑞的声音。

"放下控制。"盖博瑞提醒他。

他感觉很沮丧,问盖博瑞:"哦,你喜欢这个发型吗?"

妈妈以为这个问题是问她的,就和盖博瑞同时回答:"是的，我喜欢。"

杰森在对新发型不舒服的感觉和放下控制之间来回挣扎着。盖博瑞告诉他如果他能闭上眼睛，放下对以往长头发的回忆，会有些帮助。当杰森跟随着哥哥的建议闭上眼睛时，盖博瑞解释道，正是他对以往发型的执着才造成了他的混乱。

"现在睁开你的眼睛。"盖博瑞继续说，"没有了旧影像在你的头脑里，再看看你自己，那时再决定你是否喜欢你所看到的。"

杰森慢慢睁开眼睛，看到镜子里的自己时，愤怒消退了。他微笑着意识到他其实真的很喜欢这个新造型。

盖博瑞又提醒他一件事："这样不只是看上去很棒，而且在夏天留短发也会让你更舒服。"

杰森现在高兴了。盖博瑞绝对正确，在炎热的夏季，汗湿的头发都黏在脖子上了，这真的让他很不舒服，而现在这个发型绝对不会出现这个问题。

他悄悄对盖博瑞说了声谢谢，而妈妈却回答："不用谢，亲爱的。"

那一天余下的时间里，杰森在盖博瑞的帮助下练习放下控制，让他的高级智慧指导他的生活，因此，他经历了许多精彩的事情。

第二天醒来时，他问盖博瑞是否能继续放下控制的练习协议，因为他每天都想拥有精彩的经历。

盖博瑞满怀爱意地回答："当然，我的兄弟，当然。"

第二十八天·第二十八个故事
我在所有的事情里只看见爱和光

另一个美丽的周末,杰森的父母带他去圣地亚哥动物园。杰森以前没去过那个动物园,所以在驾车前往公园的途中他一直听着爸爸介绍。

"那个银背的大猩猩必须看,特别是这个品种已经濒临灭绝了。"爸爸说,"生活在那个动物园的猩猩是世界上仅存的一百只左右中的一只。"

他们到达时,杰森立刻兴奋地跳下车跑向入口,把父母远远地甩在了身后,父母在售票厅追上杰森,三个人一起走

进了动物园。

大约漫步了一小时，在欣赏了美丽的动物，享受了阳光之后，他们来到了银背大猩猩的展馆。在展馆前，杰森注意到展馆里的草地上方有一个壁台，离地大约八英尺高。

他身旁站着一对亚洲夫妇正在用外语互相交谈着，他们说得非常快，看起来惊慌失措。

这对夫妇指着壁台和下面的草地。杰森向下看去，看到一个大约四岁的小男孩坐在草地上，他是在看大猩猩时从栏杆上掉下去的。男孩没有受伤，但是受了惊吓，哭得很厉害。

"下去安慰他，杰森。"盖博瑞说。

杰森瞠目结舌地回答："什么？你疯了？"他不敢相信地问盖博瑞。

"哦，你是个很棒的运动员，"盖博瑞继续说，"你可以毫无问题地跳下去。"

杰森站在护栏前，他的父母在他身后几英尺的地方，他们都没有注意到掉进猩猩馆的小男孩，他们正忙着欣赏坐在洞穴区岩石上的一只大猩猩。

杰森看了看大猩猩，觉得他看上去不太友善。"似乎很危险。"他悄悄对盖博瑞说。

"哦，杰森，"盖博瑞回答，"我会把你带入危险境地吗？"随后他提醒杰森在黄石公园露营时遇到狼的事儿。

"就保持镇静。"盖博瑞告诉他，"记住你和所有生命都是连接的，那个大猩猩不会伤害你。还有，我恰好知道它实际上是一只非常友善的大猩猩。它和许多人接触过，决不会伤害任何人。所以相信我，兄弟，并且要知道无条件的爱一直在你生活里运作着。"

杰森还没意识到自己在做什么之前，已经跟随着盖博瑞的指引翻过护栏，跳到了下面的草地，他双脚安全着陆。

爸爸和妈妈惊恐地看着杰森消失在壁台另一边，他们跑过来看究竟发生了什么。

"杰森！"爸爸从上面大声喊着，"你在干吗？"

杰森抬头看着爸爸向他保证："没事的，爸爸，这个小家伙需要帮助。"

随后杰森转向小男孩，他对杰森的到来大吃一惊，立刻停止了哭泣，瞪着这个前来救他的男孩。

杰森坐下来，用手臂环绕着小男孩。"没事的，小家伙。"他温柔地说道。

小男孩用胳膊绕着杰森的脖子，爬到他的腿上。杰森轻轻揉着他的后背安慰他。"没事的，小家伙。只要我在这儿，那个大猩猩就不会伤害你。"小男孩看上去安静多了，杰森在这儿他感到很安心。

杰森向四周看看准备爬上去，但他意识到没有地方可以爬。也许是为了防止大猩猩爬出去，墙壁很陡，而壁台又很高，杰森根本够不着。

他保持冷静，是盖博瑞引领他来到这儿，他绝对会安全地带他们离开。

"现在怎么办？"他问哥哥。

"就是放松。"盖博瑞告诉他。

杰森环顾四周。"天哪！这可真不靠谱。"他想着，"我坐在大猩猩的地盘里，带着个吓坏了的四岁小孩儿，旁边还有一只长毛吓人的大猩猩，而他只是让我放松。"

突然，大猩猩站起来慢慢走向杰森和小男孩，那股熟悉的恐惧感再次侵入杰森的头脑,但他拒绝让它进来。

"爱包围着我,"他提醒自己,"我是安全的。"

这时,一小群人在护栏边聚集过来看发生了什么。没有人,包括爸爸和妈妈也不像杰森一样确信这只大猩猩不会伤害他,每个人看上去都惊慌失措。杰森知道他必须做点儿什么,好让他们知道他并不害怕。

他抱着小男孩站起来,转向人群。"没事的,"他向他们喊道,"我会照顾这个小家伙,而那只大猩猩不会伤害我们的。"

他的自信看来安慰到了他的父母,并且感动了其他人,他们开始鼓掌,赞赏他的勇敢。

杰森转向大猩猩,它现在离他们只有几英尺远。

"刚果!"一个声音突然从洞穴区传来。

杰森越过大猩猩,看见管理员正站在大猩猩早先坐着的那块石头旁边。

"刚果!"他重复道,同时走向大猩猩,"别碰那些男孩!"

男人来到大猩猩身旁,抓住它的胳膊把他拉开,杰森问:"我能摸摸他吗?"

管理员回答:"哦,我宁愿你不这么干,这个家伙喜欢玩,它也许会跟着你到处走。"

"哦。"杰森轻声回答。他仍然抱着小男孩,走向男人和大猩猩站的地方。"就摸一下。"然后伸出手开始轻轻抚摸大猩猩的头。

男人开始只是微笑着,接着就笑出了声,同时,上方的人群也爆发出笑声并再次鼓掌。

那个小男孩觉得他现在没危险了,于是也伸手去摸了摸大猩猩。

人群越发笑个不停,杰森听见他们喊:"干得好!"

管理员仍然微笑地看着杰森说:"孩子,你下来救这个小男孩真是太勇敢了,你的父母一定很为你骄傲。他们在这儿吗?"

杰森点点头,指向父母,他们还站在壁台上,看着他们的儿子成为一个英雄。

"过来,我送你们两个出去。"男人边说边把大猩猩也送回了洞穴。

杰森把小男孩放在地上,牵着他的手,跟着管理员走出了大猩猩馆,来到家人等着的地方。

小男孩看到他的父母时,松开杰森的手跑进妈妈的怀抱。他的父母拥抱亲吻着他,充满喜悦。

杰森的父母也走了过来,他们俩摇头微笑着说:"你是一个勇敢的男孩,伙计。"爸爸给了他一个大大的拥抱。

妈妈感动得说不出话来,边流泪边给了杰森一个拥抱。

杰森看向小男孩和他的家人,小男孩的父母示意他过去,杰森的父母和他一起走过去。

小男孩的妈妈搂着他,示意他看前方,她的丈夫正拿着相机站在那儿,她想和杰森合个影。

杰森非常兴奋，对着镜头微笑了。接下来，换丈夫和杰森照相。然后，他们和杰森还有被救的小男孩一块合影。

最后，照完照片，两家人挥手道别。在他们走开前，管理员跑过来递给每个家庭一些动物园的免费门票，还有可以在动物园的任何餐厅吃午餐和晚餐的免费餐券。他感谢杰森的勇敢，并说他希望再次在动物园见到杰森和他的家人。

杰森和父母继续完成他们在动物园的旅程，他们都觉得那一天不可能再有什么比大猩猩馆的经历更激动人心了！

妈妈现在平静下来，转向她的丈夫说："亲爱的，我不知道杰森身上发生了什么事，但是我真的喜欢他这样。"

"我也是。"爸爸回答，同时轻轻揉了揉儿子的头发，告诉杰森他拥有如此多的爱。

那一刻，杰森意识到，无论做什么事，只要跟随盖博瑞的指引，就会拥有彻底的喜悦和精彩的体验。

第二十九天·第二十九个故事
我感谢一切

本学期最后一天放学很早,杰森愉快地和朋友们道别,他知道在暑假期间也有机会见到他们。

他手里拿着成绩单,一路跑回家。他都等不及要给妈妈看他科科全 A,她会多高兴啊!

杰森回到家,发现妈妈留了一张字条,说她出去买东西了,很快会回来。杰森把成绩单放在厨房的桌子上,这样妈妈一进来就能看到。然后他决定给自己做些点心，晚餐之前还有好几个小时。奶酪葡萄是他的最爱！

杰森坐在餐桌前，一边享受他的点心，一边愉快地看着他那卓越的成绩单，他非常感恩。虽然他确实花了很多时间学习并按时完成学校的功课，但同时也意识到他成功的真正原因是源于盖博瑞的指引和帮助。盖博瑞教他如何对功课负责，无论何时需要，都敞开接受所有需要的信息，并且知道和接纳他值得拥有所有精彩的事物这个实相。

杰森想要向盖博瑞表达他的感激，于是他喊道："哥哥，我们谈谈！这儿没有别人，只有我们。"

杰森静静地等着盖博瑞的回应。他感觉到微风轻拂着他的脸庞，随后听见盖博瑞的声音非常近地响起。

"是的，我亲爱的兄弟。"盖博瑞说，"我们谈谈吧。"

"我想要感谢你，盖博瑞，"杰森开始说，"自从你开始指引我，我的生活就过得如此精彩！我非常感谢你教我聆听我内在的声音，并且向内寻找我需要的每一样东西。"

盖博瑞回应道："你知道每个人都有一个像我这样的高级智慧和他们在一起，但是大多数人忙于向外寻求指引，他们不聆听他们内在的指引。我亲爱的兄弟，因为你敞开聆听我的声音，并听取我的指引，这样我才能够和你交流。"

"还有，杰森。"盖博瑞又说，"我想要你知道些别的。在我进入你的生活之前，有另外一个天使指导你。你那时不知道，因为你没有敞开聆听。当我向那个天使解释说我承诺要指引你时，他就同意让我接替他。而如果我不在，将会有别的天使接替我。"

在盖博瑞说话时，杰森感觉到围绕着他的爱是如此强大，他感动地哭了起来，泪水哗哗地淌着，就好像自来水从水龙头里流出来似的。

"我希望，"他抽泣着说，"所有人都能听到他们的天使，这样他们就会和我一样快乐。"

盖博瑞轻柔地回答："别担心，杰森。将来会有一个时间，所有人都准备好聆听他们内在的指引，并感受到和你同样的快乐。你的任务是享受你的快乐，并和每个人分享。"

那一刻，杰森听到妈妈的车开进车道。他迅速擦掉眼泪，从桌边站起来，去门口迎接她。

看到爸爸也回来了，他非常激动，这样可以同时给他们看他的成绩单了。

当杰森看到他的父母对他的成功是那么高兴时，他再一次感谢盖博瑞的指引。

第三十天·第三十个故事
我整天听到爱的声音

一个星期天的下午,杰森正在家里看电视,爸爸走进来,脸上的表情很严肃。他在杰森身边坐下来说:"我们需要谈谈。"

杰森一开始感觉不太舒服,但接下来爸爸向他微笑着,用手臂搂着他的肩膀,他知道没有什么不好的事情。

杰森放松下来说:"当然,爸爸。什么事?"

"哦,儿子。"爸爸开始说,"有些事情我不明白,我想让你给我解释一下。"

爸爸继续说着,告诉杰森他绝对不是抱怨,但最近杰森身上发生的接二连三的精彩的事好得不像是真的。

"无论你做什么,结果总是完美。"他说,"甚至当情况对我来说都不确定的时候,你总是精确地知道要做什么。"

杰森完全知道爸爸在说什么。自从盖博瑞教他聆听内在的指引,他的生活就变成了一个不可思议的,精彩纷呈的旅程,而这对每个人来说都是很明显的。

他安静地坐在那儿。爸爸继续说:"还有,你看起来总是在和什么人交谈，然而实际上又什么人都没有。"这时他紧张地笑起来，"简直就像有一个看不见的精灵或是其他什么东西跟随着你。"

杰森和爸爸一起笑起来，突然听见了盖博瑞的声音。

"你想要告诉他，是吧？"盖博瑞问。

"嗯，嗯。"杰森在笑声的间歇中含糊地说。

"那好，说吧。"盖博瑞告诉他，"反正他也不会相信你，但是去试试吧。"

杰森止住笑声，脸上浮现出一个巨大的微笑，他突然感到无比自由。

"爸爸，"在盖博瑞改变主意之前，他迅速说，"我告诉你一直以来发生在我身上的事。"

爸爸往后坐坐，背靠着沙发，看着儿子，全神贯注地低声说道："说吧。"

杰森慢慢地说道："是盖博瑞，爸爸。他仍然和我在一起。在他离开身体之前，我们做了一个约定，我们两人中谁先离开，就会和另一个待在一起指导他。盖博瑞就是我的精灵，你也可以称他为我的天使。"

爸爸抬了抬眉毛，又皱了一下额头："你不愿意告诉我真正发生了什么，是吗，杰森？"他问。

盖博瑞是对的，爸爸不相信他。杰森回答："听好，爸爸，盖博瑞整天都和我说话。他告诉我做什么，去哪里，去见谁，还有跟他们说什么，他保护我远离所有危险。我告诉你，爸爸，他时刻和我在一起，每一天都在一起。"

"那么他现在也和你在一起吗？"爸爸怀疑地问道。

"是的，他在这儿，但只有我能听到他的声音。"杰森抬起头，好像在听着别人都听不到的什么东西。

然后他说："他想要告诉你一些事，爸爸。"

"真的？"爸爸说，现在他看上去似乎燃起了希望，"是什么？"

"哦，"杰森开始说，"他想要你知道，你也有一个天使在指引你，每个人都有。但是当你忙着向外寻求指引和答案的时候，你听不到你的天使的声音。你必须聆听你自己内在的声音。"

杰森停顿了一下，让爸爸想一下他所说的。然后继续说道："你有一个天使名叫艾萨克，他一直试着和你交流。请进入内在，聆听他，他有很多话要告诉你。"

爸爸不知道自己要想些什么。尽管他对杰森的解释感觉很和平，但他还不确定已经准备好接受他自己的天使了。他感谢杰森和他分享这些，并且告诉杰森，他相信他，而且很高兴盖博瑞的指引使他的生活如此完美。

"然而我不认为我已经准备好跟随我的天使了。"爸爸承认道，"我想我还要继续靠自己做事情，直到我准备好聆听我内在的指引。"

尽管杰森有点儿失望，爸爸还没准备好聆听他自己的天使，他还是非常高兴爸爸能理解盖博瑞的事，那样他就再也不用掩饰什么了。

爸爸侧过身拥抱着杰森说："杰森，我爱你。继续保持这样。"然后站起身，微笑着走出房间，上楼告诉妻子他和儿子的这次谈话。

"我很高兴你是我的天使和伙伴。"杰森告诉盖博瑞。

"我也是。"盖博瑞回应道，"有个兄弟在身体里，可以和他一起玩，又可以指引他，真是太好了。"

杰森微笑着，感到和平和爱的暖流涌上心头，他默默感谢他的天使——盖博瑞。

奇迹日记

永远记得彼尚的法则：每一件"可以"发生的事终将"会"发生。期待奇迹！

第一天·第一个故事 | 我观察我说了什么

肯定语句：我只为和平而说话。

谨记今天 信守承诺

第二天·第二个故事 | 我留意我听到了什么

肯定语句：我只为和平而聆听。

谨记今天 信守承诺

第三天·第三个故事 | 我觉察我看到了什么

肯定语句：我到处都能看到和平。

谨记今天 信守承诺

第四天 · 第四个故事　　我并不知道我所看见的真正意义

肯定语句：和平围绕着我。

谨记今天 信守承诺

第五天 · 第五个故事　　我愿意看见光

肯定语句：我只认识内在的和平。

谨记今天 信守承诺

第六天 · 第六个故事　　我警醒于光

肯定语句：我警醒于光。

谨记今天 信守承诺

第七天·第七个故事　　　我非常富足

_____
_____
_____

肯定语句：我是如此和平。

谨记今天 信守承诺

第八天·第八个故事 　　每个人都希望为我贡献

_____
_____
_____

肯定语句：我在每个人的行动中都能看到和平。

谨记今天 信守承诺

第九天·第九个故事 　　　我值得富足

_____
_____
_____

肯定语句：我的星球值得和平。

谨记今天 信守承诺

第十天·第十个故事　　我敞开接受宇宙所有的礼物

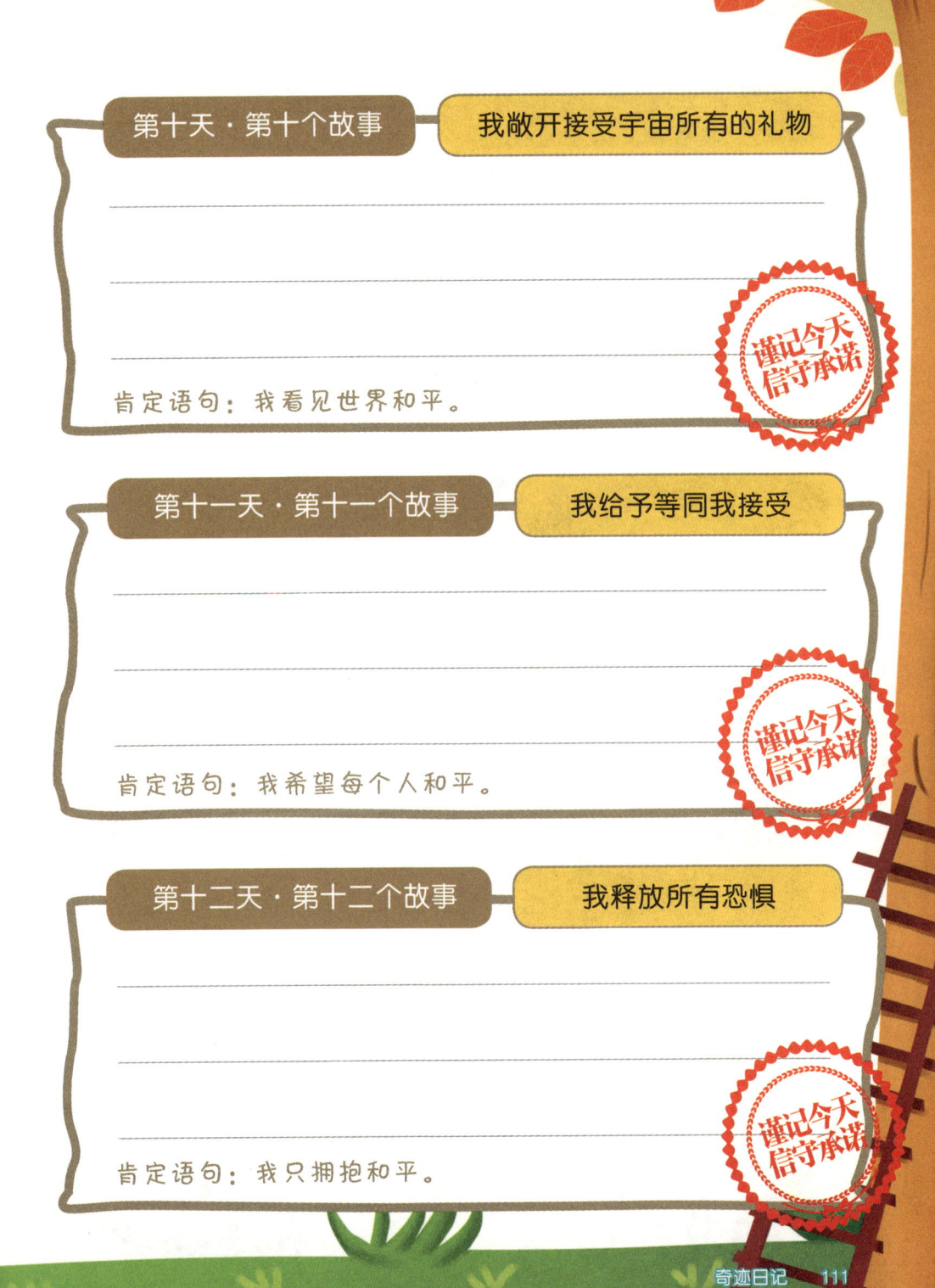

肯定语句：我看见世界和平。

谨记今天 信守承诺

第十一天·第十一个故事　　我给予等同我接受

肯定语句：我希望每个人和平。

谨记今天 信守承诺

第十二天·第十二个故事　　我释放所有恐惧

肯定语句：我只拥抱和平。

谨记今天 信守承诺

第十三天·第十三个故事   我敞开心扉走向和平

肯定语句：我向和平敞开我的生活。

第十四天·第十四个故事   我认出我的最佳利益

肯定语句：和平是我唯一的渴望。

第十五天·第十五个故事   我有耐心

肯定语句：和平是永恒的。

第十六天·第十六个故事 | **做出反应前，我暂停片刻**

肯定语句：我爱和平。

谨记今天 信守承诺

第十七天·第十七个故事 | **我敞开接受奇迹**

肯定语句：我看到每个人都和平。

谨记今天 信守承诺

第十八天·第十八个故事 | **我只选择和平**

肯定语句：我爱我的和平。

谨记今天 信守承诺

第十九天·第十九个故事　　我充满爱,我值得被爱

肯定语句:和平照耀着我。

谨记今天 信守承诺

第二十天·第二十个故事　　只有爱存在,恐惧是幻象

肯定语句:和平在我心里。

谨记今天 信守承诺

第二十一天·第二十一个故事　　父亲无条件地爱着我

肯定语句:此刻我感觉到和平。

谨记今天 信守承诺

第二十二天·第二十二个故事　　父亲爱我比我爱自己更多

肯定语句：和平与我合一。

第二十三天·第二十三个故事　　我信任我的父亲

肯定语句：我信任和平。

第二十四天·第二十四个故事　　我父亲很伟大，我也是

肯定语句：和平是伟大的。

第二十五天·第二十五个故事 　　我放手，让父亲指引我

肯定语句：我照耀和平。

谨记今天 信守承诺

第二十六天·第二十六个故事 　　作为宇宙之子，我是有福的

肯定语句：我有宇宙的和平。

谨记今天 信守承诺

第二十七天·第二十七个故事 　　今天属于我的高级智慧

肯定语句：我与和平合一。

谨记今天 信守承诺

第二十八天 · 第二十八个故事　　我在所有的事情上只看见爱与光

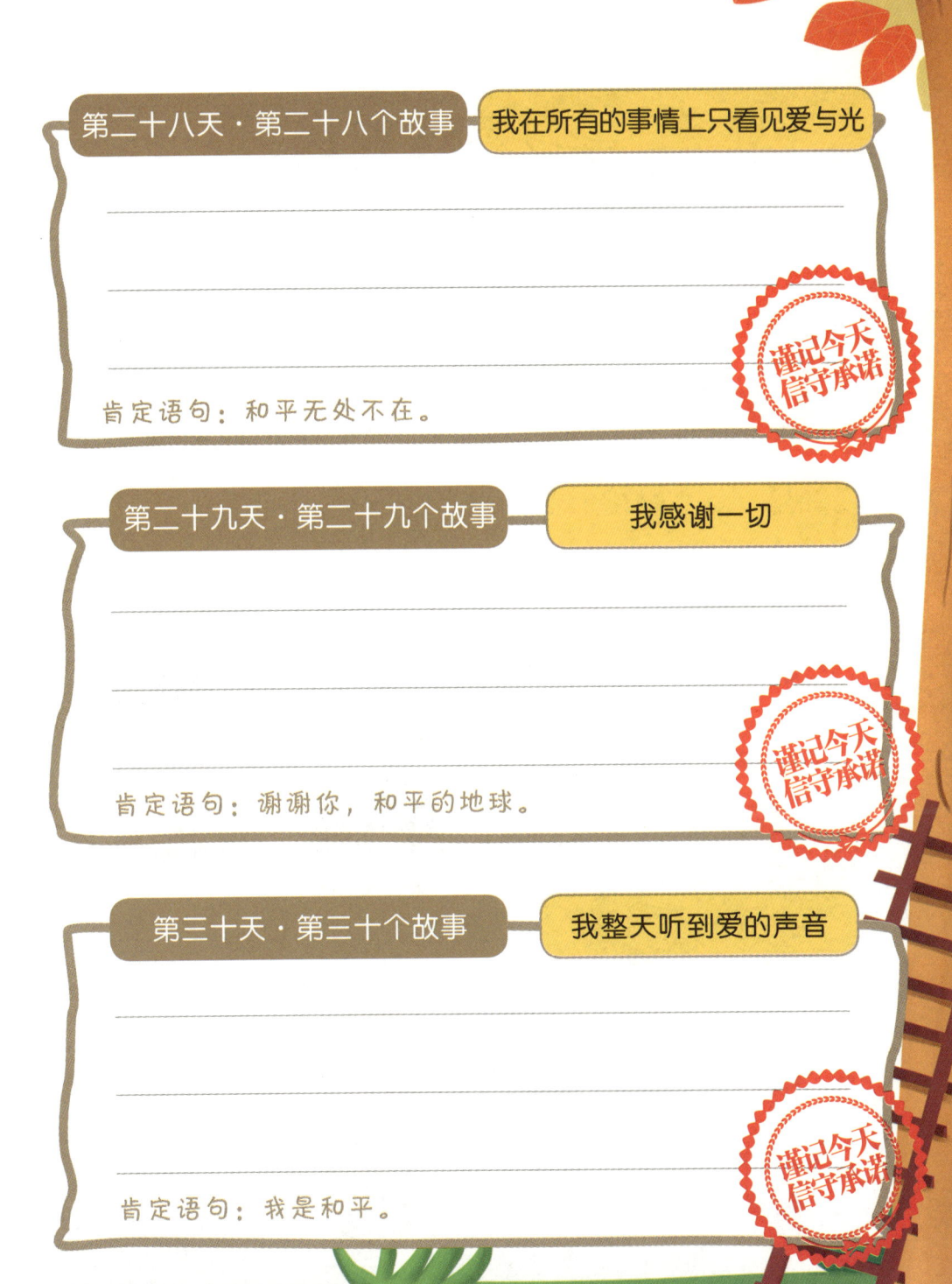

肯定语句：和平无处不在。

第二十九天 · 第二十九个故事　　我感谢一切

肯定语句：谢谢你，和平的地球。

第三十天 · 第三十个故事　　我整天听到爱的声音

肯定语句：我是和平。

后记

我给予所有的孩子我的祝福，无论你们是什么年纪。这不是你旅程的终点，而是你成长的开始！

敞开心扉去接受所有的可能性，并且谨记：你的真正身份跟你认为自己是什么并没有关系，但是你外在发生的一切，正是你如何认定自己的结果。

EPILOGUE

To all the children, whatever their age, I send my blessings. This is not an end to your experience, but rather the beginning of your growth.

Always be open to the possibilities, and remember — who you are has nothing to do with what you think of yourself, but everything that happens outside of you is a direct result of what you think of yourself.

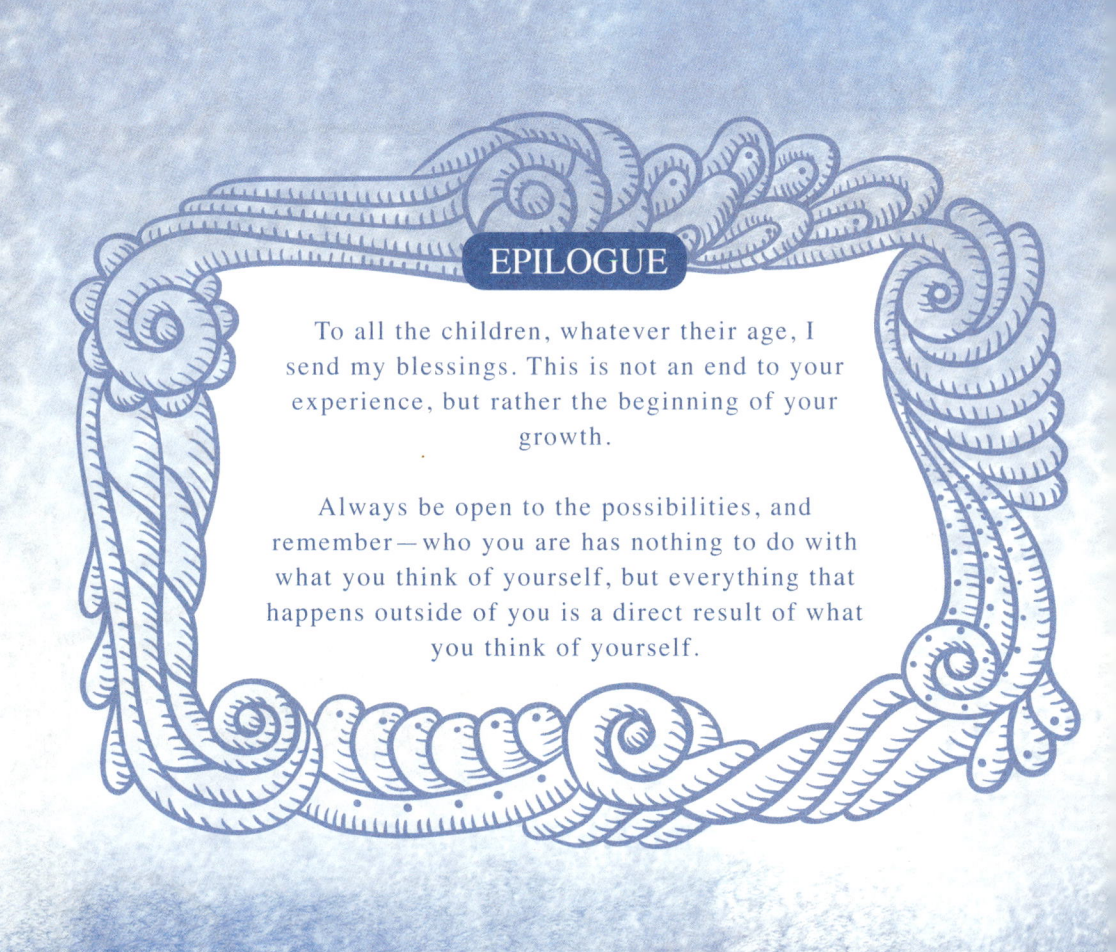

Day 28 ~ Story 28

I See Only Love and Light In All My Affairs

_____

_____

_____

_____

Affirmation: *Peace is everywhere.*

REMEMBER TO KEEP YOUR WORD TODAY

Day 29 ~ Story 29

I Am Thankful

_____

_____

_____

_____

Affirmation: *Thank you, peaceful Earth.*

REMEMBER TO KEEP YOUR WORD TODAY

Day 30 ~ Story 30

I Hear the Voice of Love All Day

_____

_____

_____

_____

Affirmation: *I am peace.*

REMEMBER TO KEEP YOUR WORD TODAY

Day 25 ~ Story 25

**I Let Go
And Let My Father Be My Guide**

_____
_____
_____
_____

Affirmation: *I shine peace.*

REMEMBER TO KEEP YOUR WORD TODAY

Day 26 ~ Story 26

**I Am Blessed
As a Child of the Universe**

_____
_____
_____
_____

Affirmation: *I have the peace of the universe.*

REMEMBER TO KEEP YOUR WORD TODAY

Day 27 ~ Story 27

**Today Belongs to My
Higher Self**

_____
_____
_____
_____

Affirmation: *I am one with peace.*

REMEMBER TO KEEP YOUR WORD TODAY

Day 22 ~ Story 22

My Father Loves Me More Than I Love Myself

Affirmation: *Peace and I are one.*

REMEMBER TO KEEP YOUR WORD TODAY

Day 23 ~ Story 23

I Trust My Father

Affirmation: *I trust peace.*

REMEMBER TO KEEP YOUR WORD TODAY

Day 24 ~ Story 24

My Father Is Great And So Am I

Affirmation: *Peace is great.*

REMEMBER TO KEEP YOUR WORD TODAY

Day 19 ~ Story 19 | **I Am Loving and Lovable**

Affirmation: *Peace shines upon me.*

REMEMBER TO KEEP YOUR WORD TODAY

Day 20 ~ Story 20 | **Only Love Exists– Fear Is an Illusion**

Affirmation: *Peace is within me.*

REMEMBER TO KEEP YOUR WORD TODAY

Day 21 ~ Story 21 | **My Father Loves Me Unconditionally**

Affirmation: *I feel peace now.*

REMEMBER TO KEEP YOUR WORD TODAY

Day 16 ~ Story 16　　　**I Pause Before I React**

_____

_____

_____

Affirmation: *I love peace.*

REMEMBER TO KEEP YOUR WORD TODAY

Day 17 ~ Story 17　　　**I Am Open To Receive Miracles**

_____

_____

_____

Affirmation: *I see everyone peaceful.*

REMEMBER TO KEEP YOUR WORD TODAY

Day 18 ~ Story 18　　　**I Choose Only Peace**

_____

_____

_____

Affirmation: *I love my peace.*

REMEMBER TO KEEP YOUR WORD TODAY

Day 13 ~ Story 13 — I Open My Mind to Peace

Affirmation: *I open my life to peace.*

REMEMBER TO KEEP YOUR WORD TODAY

Day 14 ~ Story 14 — I Recognize My Own Best Interest

Affirmation: *Peace is all I desire.*

REMEMBER TO KEEP YOUR WORD TODAY

Day 15 ~ Story 15 — I Am Patient

Affirmation: *Peace is forever.*

REMEMBER TO KEEP YOUR WORD TODAY

Day 10 ~ Story 10 | **I Am Open To Receive All the Gifts of the Universe**

Affirmation: *I see world peace.*

REMEMBER TO KEEP YOUR WORD TODAY

Day 11 ~ Story 11 | **I Give As I Receive**

Affirmation: *I wish peace for everyone.*

REMEMBER TO KEEP YOUR WORD TODAY

Day 12 ~ Story 12 | **I Release All Fear**

Affirmation: *I embrace only peace.*

REMEMBER TO KEEP YOUR WORD TODAY

Day 7 ~ Story 7   **I Am Very Prosperous**

_____

_____

_____

Affirmation: *I am so peaceful.*

REMEMBER
TO KEEP
YOUR WORD
TODAY

Day 8 ~ Story 8   **Everyone Wishes
To Contribute to Me**

_____

_____

_____

Affirmation: *I see peace in everyone's actions.*

REMEMBER
TO KEEP
YOUR WORD
TODAY

Day 9 ~ Story 9   **I Deserve Prosperity**

_____

_____

_____

Affirmation: *My planet Earth deserves peace.*

REMEMBER
TO KEEP
YOUR WORD
TODAY

Day 4 ~ Story 4

I Do Not Know the Real Meaning Of What I See

_____

_____

_____

Affirmation: *I am surrounded by peace.*

REMEMBER TO KEEP YOUR WORD TODAY

Day 5 ~ Story 5

I Am Willing To See the Light

_____

_____

_____

Affirmation: *I know only peace inside.*

REMEMBER TO KEEP YOUR WORD TODAY

Day 6 ~ Story 6

I Will Stay in the Light

_____

_____

_____

Affirmation: *I am vigilant for peace.*

REMEMBER TO KEEP YOUR WORD TODAY

| Day 1 ~ Story 1 | I Watch What I Say |

_____
_____
_____
_____

Affirmation: *I speak only for peace.*

REMEMBER TO KEEP YOUR WORD TODAY

| Day 2 ~ Story 2 | I Notice What I Hear |

_____
_____
_____
_____

Affirmation: *I listen only for peace.*

REMEMBER TO KEEP YOUR WORD TODAY

| Day 3 ~ Story 3 | I Am Aware of What I See |

_____
_____
_____
_____

Affirmation: *I see peace everywhere.*

REMEMBER TO KEEP YOUR WORD TODAY

30-Day
Miracle Journal

Always remember Bijan's Law:

Everything that CAN go right

WILL go right.

EXPECT MIRACLES!

"Yes, he's here, but only I can hear him." Jason stopped for a moment and cocked his head, as if listening to something unheard by anyone else.

Then he said, "He wants to tell you something, Dad."

"Really," Dad replied, seeming a bit hopeful now. "What is it?"

"Well," Jason began, "he wants you to know that you have an angel guiding you, too. Everyone does. But you can't hear your angel's voice while you're busy looking outside yourself for guidance and answers. You have to listen to the voice within yourself."

Jason paused for a moment to let his dad think about all he was saying. Then he continued, "You have a guide named Isaac, who has been trying to communicate with you. Please go within and listen to him—he has much to tell you."

Dad was not sure what to think. Although he felt very much at peace with Jason's explanation, he was not sure he was ready to accept having his very own angel. He thanked Jason for sharing this information and told him that he believed him and was glad that Gabriel's guidance was working so well in his life.

"I don't think I'm ready to follow my guide yet," Dad confessed. "I think I will have to continue doing things on my own until I am ready to listen to my inner guide."

Although Jason was a bit disappointed that his dad was not ready to listen to his own guide, he was very happy that his dad understood about Gabriel, and that he would not have to cover it up any more.

Dad leaned over to hug Jason and said, "Jason, I love you. Keep up the good work." He then stood up and smiled as he walked out of the room and up the stairs, to tell his wife about this conversation with their son.

As Jason watched his dad climb the stairs, he sat back on the couch and thanked Gabriel for giving him permission to tell their father.

"I'm glad you're my guide and companion." he told Gabriel.

"Me, too," Gabriel responded. "It's fun to have a brother in a body to play with and to guide." Jason smiled as he felt a rush of love and peace flow over him, and he silently gave thanks for his angel, Gabriel.

you always know exactly what to do."

Jason knew exactly what his dad was talking about. Since Gabriel had taught him to listen to his inner guide, his life had been transformed into a magnificent, wonderful experience. And it must have been obvious to everyone.

He sat there quietly while his dad continued.

"Also," Dad said, "it often appears that you are talking to someone when there is really nobody there." Then he laughed nervously, "It's almost like you have an invisible genie or something."

Jason laughed along with his father and suddenly heard Gabriel's voice.

"You want to tell him, don't you?" Gabriel asked.

"Uh-huh." Jason muttered in the middle of his laughter.

"All right then, go ahead," Gabriel told him. "He won't believe you anyway, but go ahead and try."

Jason stopped laughing, and a big smile spread across his face. He suddenly felt free.

"Dad," he said quickly, before Gabriel could change his mind, "I'll tell you exactly what's been going on."

Dad sat back on the couch and looked at his son. He was all ears. "Go on." he whispered.

Jason continued slowly. "It's Gabriel, Dad. He's still with me. Before he left his body, we made an agreement that whichever one of us left first would stay with the other one and guide him. Gabriel is my genie. You could also call him my angel."

Dad raised an eyebrow and frowned. "You wouldn't like to tell me what's really going on, would you, Jason?" he asked.

Gabriel was right—his dad did not believe him. Jason replied, "Listen, Dad—Gabriel talks to me all day long. He tells me what to do, where to go, who to see and what to tell them. He protects me from all danger. I'm telling you, Dad—he's with me all day, every day."

"So he's here with you now?" Dad asked doubtfully.

105

Day 30 ~ Story 30

I Hear the Voice of Love
All Day

One Sunday afternoon, as Jason was watching television in the family room, his dad walked in with a serious look on his face. He sat down on the couch next to Jason and said, "We need to talk."

Jason felt uncomfortable at first, but then his dad smiled at him and put his arm around Jason's shoulder to let Jason know that nothing was wrong.

Jason relaxed and said, "Sure, Dad. What's up?"

"Well, son," Dad began, "something is going on that I don't understand, and I'd like you to explain it to me."

Dad continued, telling Jason that he certainly was not complaining, but that the wonderful things going on with Jason lately had all seemed too good to be true.

"Whatever you do turns out perfect," he said. "Even when the situation looks uncertain to me,

could be as happy as I am."

Gabriel replied softly, "Don't worry, Jason. There will come a time when all people will be ready to listen to their inner guides and experience the same happiness that you do. Your job is to enjoy your happiness and share your joy with everyone."

At that moment, Jason heard Mom's car pull into the driveway. He quickly wiped away his tears and got up from the table to greet her at the door.

He noticed Dad pulling up at the same time, and was very excited that he would get to show his report card to both of them at once.

As Jason imagined how happy his parents would be at his success, he thanked Gabriel once more for his guidance.

When Jason arrived home, he found a note from Mom, saying she had gone shopping and would be home soon. Jason set his report card on the kitchen table so she would see it as soon as she came in. Then he decided to make a snack for himself, since he knew it would be a few hours before dinner. Cheese and grapes were his favorite!

As Jason sat at the table enjoying his snack and stating with joy at his excellent report card, he felt very thankful. It's true that he had put in a lot of time studying and doing his schoolwork, but he realized that the true source of his success at school was Gabriel's guidance and support.

Gabriel had taught him to be responsible about his schoolwork, to be open to receive all the information he needed whenever he needed it, and also to know and accept that he deserved wonderful things.

Jason wanted to express his thanks to Gabriel, so he called to him. "Brother," he called, "let's talk! Nobody's here but us."

Jason listened quietly for Gabriel to respond. He felt a soft breeze caressing his face and then heard Gabriel's voice very close by.

"Yes, my beloved brother." Gabriel said. "Let's talk."

"I want to thank you, Gabriel," Jason began. "Since you have been guiding me, my life has been so wonderful! I am so thankful that you taught me to listen to my inner voice and to look within myself for everything I need."

Gabriel responded, "You know that everyone has a guide like me with them, but most people are so busy looking outside themselves for guidance, they don't listen to their inner guide. My beloved brother, it is because you are open to hearing my voice and listening to my guidance that I am able to communicate with you."

"And Jason," Gabriel added, "I would like you to know something else. You had another angel guiding you before I got here. You did not know it then, because you were not open to listening. When I explained to the other angel that I had promised to guide you, he agreed to allow me to take his place. And if I were not around, there would be another angel to take my place."

As Gabriel spoke, the feeling of love that surrounded Jason was so powerful that he began crying. The tears flowing endlessly, like water from a faucet.

"I wish," he sobbed quietly, "that all people knew about their angels so they

Day 29 ~ Story 29

I Am Thankful

Classes were dismissed early on the last day of school. Jason said a joyous good-bye to all of his friends, knowing he would have an opportunity to see them over the summer vacation.

He ran all the way home with his report card in his hand. He could hardly wait to show his mom—she would be so happy to see that he received A's in every subject!

101

Before they parted ways, the zookeeper ran over and gave each family several free passes to the zoo and coupons for free lunch and dinner at any of the zoo's restaurants. He thanked Jason for his bravery and told him he hoped to see him and his family back at the zoo soon.

Jason and his parents continued on their way to complete their tour of the zoo, although they all agreed they couldn't possibly experience anything else that day that could be more exciting than what they experienced at the gorilla exhibit!

Mom was calm now and turned to her husband.

"Honey," she said quietly, "I don't know what's going on with Jason, but I really like it."

"Me, too." Dad replied, as he rustled his son's hair and told him how very much he was loved.

At that moment, Jason realized that as long as he followed Gabriel's guidance in everything he did, he would have totally joyous and wonderful experiences in his life.

"Come on," the man said as he began to escort the gorilla back to the cave. "Let's get you both back where you belong."

Jason set the boy on the ground and held his hand as they followed the zookeeper out of the gorilla exhibit, up to where their families were waiting.

When the boy saw his parents, he released Jason's hand and ran into his mother's arms. Both parents hugged and kissed their son with joy.

Jason's parents walked over to meet him, shaking their heads and smiling at the same time.

"You're a brave boy, buddy," Dad told him as he gave him a big hug.

Mom was too emotional to speak, and tears rolled down her face as she gave Jason a hug.

Jason looked over at the boy and his family, and the boy's parents were motioning for him to come over to them. Jason's parents walked over with him.

The boy's mother put her arm around Jason and motioned for him to look in front of them where her husband was standing with a camera. She wanted to have a photo with Jason!"

Jason got a kick out of this and he smiled just as the photo was taken. Next, it was the mother who took a photo of her husband and Jason. Then, of course, they had to have a photo of Jason with their little boy who had been rescued.

Finally all the photography was finished and the families were waving good-bye to each other.

He stood up with the boy in his arms and turned to the crowd. "It's okay," he called to them. "I'm gonna take care of this little guy, and that gorilla isn't going to touch either one of us."

His confidence seemed to comfort his parents, and to impress the rest of the group who began clapping and commenting on his bravery.

Jason turned back to the gorilla, who was now just a few feet away.

"Congo!" a voice suddenly yelled from the cave area.

Jason looked past the gorilla and saw the zookeeper standing by the rock the gorilla had been sitting on earlier.

"Congo!" he repeated, as he walked toward where the gorilla was now standing. "Leave those boys alone!"

The man then told Jason, "It's okay. He won't hurt you—he's well trained."

As the man reached the gorilla and took him by the arm to lead him away, Jason asked, "Can I pet him?"

The zookeeper replied, "Well, I'd rather you didn't. This guy loves to play, and he might try to follow you everywhere."

"Oh," Jason replied softly. Still holding the boy in his arms, he walked over to where the man stood with the gorilla. "Just a little?" he asked, as he reached out his hand and began petting the gorilla's head.

The man smiled and began to chuckle, and at the same time the crowd above broke into laughter and began clapping again.

The little boy could sense there was no danger and he, too, reached out to pet the gorilla.

This threw the crowd into another fit of laughter, and Jason heard them shouting, "Bravo!"

Still smiling, the zookeeper looked at Jason and said, "Son, it was very brave of you to come down here to save the boy. Your parents would be very proud of you. Are they here?"

Jason nodded and pointed up to where his parents were still standing on the ledge watching their son become a hero.

"Jason!" Dad screamed from up above. "What are you doing?"

Jason looked up at his dad and assured him, "It's okay, Dad. This little guy needs help."

Then Jason turned to the boy, who was so startled by Jason's arrival that he stopped crying immediately, and could only stare at the young man who had come to save him.

Jason sat down and put his arms around the boy. "It's okay, little guy," he said gently.

The boy threw his arms around Jason's neck and climbed into his lap. Jason rubbed the boy's back and comforted him. "It's okay, buddy. That gorilla won't hurt you as long as I'm here." The boy seemed calmer now, comforted by Jason being there.

As Jason looked around for a way to climb out, he realized that there was none. The wall below the ledge had been cut back about three feet, probably to prevent the gorillas from climbing out, and the ledge itself was too high for him to reach.

He remained calm, remembering that Gabriel had led him here and would surely lead him safely out.

"Now what?" he asked his brother.

"Just relax." Gabriel told him.

Jason looked around. "That's great." he thought,

"I'm sitting in a gorilla pit with a frightened four-year-old and a hairy, scary-looking gorilla, and he wants me to just relax. Jeez!"

Suddenly the gorilla stood up and began walking slowly toward Jason and the boy. That old fear tried to creep into Jason's mind again, but he refused to buy into it.

"Love surrounds me," he reminded himself. "I am safe."

By this time, a small group of people had gathered at the railing to see what was going on. No one, including Mom and Dad, was as certain about the gorilla as Jason was—everyone seemed to be in a panic. Jason knew he had to do something to let them know he was not afraid.

and the sunshine, they reached the silverback gorilla exhibit. The family approached the exhibit and Jason noticed a ledge that dropped down about eight feet onto a grassy area inside the exhibit. Standing next to him were an Asian man and woman speaking to each other in a foreign language. They spoke very quickly and appeared to be in a panic.

The Asian couple began pointing over the ledge to the grassy area below. Jason looked down and saw a little boy about four years old, who had fallen over the railing while looking at the gorillas. The boy sat on the grass, unharmed but very afraid and crying loudly.

"Go down there and comfort him, Jason." Gabriel said.

Jason was stunned. "What? Are you crazy?" he asked Gabriel in disbelief.

"Oh, come on, you're an excellent athlete," Gabriel continued. "You could jump right down there with no trouble at all."

Jason stood at the railing with his parents a few feet behind him; they had not yet noticed the little boy who had fallen into the gorilla exhibit. They were busy admiring one of the gorillas that was sitting on a rock near the cave area.

Jason looked at the gorilla and decided he did not look very friendly. "It looks dangerous," he said quietly to Gabriel.

"Oh Jason," Gabriel replied. "Would I lead you into a dangerous situation?" He then reminded Jason of the incident with the wolf when he was camping at Yellowstone.

"Just stay calm," Gabriel told him, "and remember your connection with all life. That gorilla will not hurt you. Besides, I happen to know that he is actually a very friendly gorilla. He has had a lot of human contact, and would never hurt anyone. So trust me, my brother, and know that Unconditional Love is working in your life all the time."

Before Jason knew what he was doing, he found himself following Gabriel's guidance. He climbed over the railing and dropped to the grass below, landing safely on both feet.

Mom and Dad watched in horror as their son disappeared over the ledge, and they ran over to see what had happened.

Day 28 ~ Story 28

I See Only Love and Light
In All My Affairs

Another beautiful weekend had arrived, and Jason's parents were taking him to the San Diego Zoo. Jason had never before been to the zoo, so during the car ride he heard all about it from his dad.

"The silverback gorilla is a must see, especially because the species is on the brink of extinction," Dad said. "The gorillas that live at the zoo are a few of only about one hundred left in the world."

When they arrived, Jason was so excited that he ran all the way from the car to the entrance, leaving his parents behind. They caught up with Jason at the ticket booth, and all three entered the park together.

After about an hour of walking around enjoying the beautiful animals

of control. Gabriel told him it would help if he would close his eyes and let go of the memory of the way he used to look with his longer hair. As Jason followed his brother's advice, Gabriel explained that it was only his attachment to the way he used to look that was causing him to struggle.

"Now open your eyes," Gabriel continued, "and look at yourself without that old image in your mind. Then decide if you like what you see."

Jason slowly opened his eyes. As he looked at his reflection, his anger faded. He smiled as he realized that he really did like the new look.

Gabriel reminded him of one more thing. "Not only does it look great, but it's going to be more comfortable for you to have short hair in the summertime, anyway."

Jason was happy now. Gabriel was absolutely right—a hairy, sweaty neck always made him uncomfortable during the heat of the summer. This haircut was going to work out great.

He quietly said thank you to Gabriel, and his mom replied, "You're welcome, honey."

As they were leaving the salon, Jason grabbed his mom's hand and told her she was the best mom in the world.

"I really love you, Mom," he said.

Mom squeezed his hand and replied, "I love you, too, Jason."

For the remainder of the day, with Gabriel's help, Jason practiced giving up control and letting his higher self direct his life, and he experienced many wonderful things because of it.

When he awoke the next day, he asked Gabriel if it was okay for him to continue his agreement to give up control, because he wanted to have wonderful experiences every day.

Gabriel lovingly replied, "Of course, my brother, of course."

ready.

A few minutes later, a lady named Julie came to the lobby to tell Jason she would be filling in for Greg. She motioned for Jason to follow her, so she could begin washing his hair.

Jason felt uncomfortable about a lady cutting his hair. He was about to protest when Gabriel said, "You agreed to give up control." Remembering his agreement, he decided to let his higher self control the situation. He stood up and followed Julie back to the sink.

After the wash, Jason sat in Julie's chair, and she began working on his hair. He loved getting his hair cur because it was so relaxing to feel someone playing with his hair.

He was so relaxed that he dozed off, and woke up to the sound of the blow dryer. Rubbing his eyes, he looked in the mirror as Julie dried his hair. As he watched, he noticed that he looked very different. Julie had cut his hair much shorter than he had worn it before. He was shocked and could only stare at his unfamiliar reflection.

About five minutes later, Julie put the blow dryer down, removed the plastic smock from around his neck and said, "You're all done, sport."

Jason turned away from the mirror and looked over at his mom, who had been waiting nearby. "Wow!" she exclaimed. "What a handsome boy! What do you think?" she asked.

"Mom," Jason gasped, "she cut off all my hair!"

Mom replied, "Well, it is much shorter, but, honey, it looks really good. I like it!"

Jason was about to say something harsh to Julie, until he heard Gabriel's voice again.

"Let go of control." Gabriel reminded him.

Feeling very upset, he asked Gabriel, "Well, do you like it?"

Mom thought the question was directed at her, and answered the same time as Gabriel. Jason heard them both say, "Yes, I do."

Jason was struggling between his feelings about the haircut, and letting go

Gabriel continued, "Come on, wake up, it's a beautiful morning!"

Jason grabbed his pillow and covered his ears.

This threw Gabriel into a fit of laughter. "Those covers can't keep me out! My voice will always be in your head!"

Jason was awake by now, and he grinned, throwing the covers off to get some fresh air.

"Are you ever going to show yourself again?" he asked Gabriel. "Or am I only going to hear you forever?"

"Right now, you'll just hear me, but when the time is right, you'll see me, too," Gabriel said.

Jason was glad to know that someday he would see Gabriel again.

"So," he began, "what's up? Why are you waking me so early on a Saturday? It's my day to sleep in!"

"Well, today is going to be a very special day," Gabriel replied. "Today, I want you to let go of the need to control things that are happening in your life. I want you to give that control to me and your higher self, and trust us to bring you a wonderful day."

Jason did not really understand Gabriel's request. He did not think he was trying to control events in his life, but Gabriel assured him that even though we don't realize it, we are always trying to be in control.

"It is when we give control to our Higher Selves," Gabriel told him, "that we always experience the wonderful things the universe has in store for us."

Jason agreed to be aware of giving up control, and Gabriel said he would help him.

After breakfast that morning, Mom informed Jason that he had an appointment to get his hair cut at 9:30 a.m., which was about half an hour away. Jason got ready, and he and his mom arrived at the salon just in time.

After checking in at the appointment desk, Jason discovered that his hairdresser, Greg, had called the salon to say he would be at work an hour late that morning, so another hairdresser would be filling in for him. Jason and his mom were asked to wait in the lobby until the fill-in hairdresser was

Day 27 ~ Story 27

Today Belongs to My Higher Self

One Saturday morning, Jason woke up to hear his brother Gabriel's voice joyously singing, "Good morning, sunshine, it's time to get up!"

Jason groaned and rolled over, pulling the covers over his head.

Jason didn't appreciate, it was his big,

juicy kisses. But Uncle John sure loved giving them.

Uncle John reached into his pocket and pulled out his wallet. "I've got something for you, buddy," he told Jason, as he knelt down to Jason's height and handed his nephew a one hundred dollar bill.

"A hundred dollars!" Jason exclaimed. "Wow! Thanks, Uncle John!" He threw his arms around his uncle's neck, giving him a big hug, all the while thinking about all the cool stuff he was going to buy.

As he pulled away, his uncle looked at him and said, "Jason, I want you to know you are my favorite nephew, and I really love you. I feel very blessed to have you in my life, because you are such a wonderful boy."

Jason could feel his uncle's unconditional love surrounding him. He turned to look at his parents, who stood with their arms around each other, smiling at their son, and he realized how very blessed he was to have such a loving family that cared so much for him.

The front door suddenly burst open and out came Jason's two cousins, racing to see who would get to greet him first. He smiled, feeling blessed again that his loving family extended beyond his wonderful parents.

After a wonderful dinner and then a fireworks celebration at Uncle John's, Jason and his parents headed home. As he lay down to sleep, he was thankful for being blessed with such a loving family. "Gabriel," he asked, "is everyone blessed with a wonderful family?"

Gabriel told him, "Yes, but not everyone is aware of it, as you are. And Jason, if you don't know you have something, it really doesn't do you any good—it's almost like not having it at all."

"But you," he continued, "you are always aware of the many blessings in your life. Not only do you see them everywhere, you create even more blessings by being so thankful for them."

"You taught me how to do that, Gabriel," Jason replied sleepily. "You are one of my blessings," he said as he drifted off to sleep, "and I'm very thankful for you, too."

Day 26 ~ Story 26

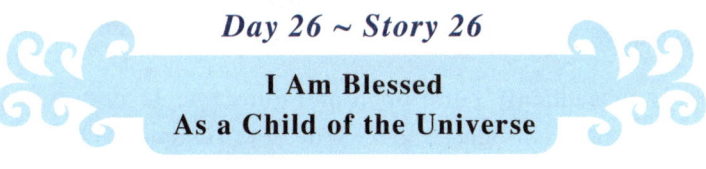

I Am Blessed
As a Child of the Universe

Jason's Uncle John was having a small dinner party at his house, to celebrate the Fourth of July. Jason really liked Uncle John. He was always jolly and had a great sense of humor. Uncle John's jokes always made him laugh. He was generous, too. He always had a gift for Jason—a shirt, a game, and sometimes even money.

The short drive to Uncle John's was over—they had arrived. Jason rang the doorbell, and they were greeted by Uncle John's smiling face. He stepped outside to welcome his family, hugging his sister-in-law and brother, and picking Jason up to give him a big squeeze and a kiss on the cheek.

"Wow!" exclaimed Uncle John. "It seems like you've grown a foot since I last saw you, buddy!"

As Uncle John set him down on the ground, Jason laughed and wiped at the wetness of his Uncle's kiss. If there was anything about Uncle John that

Jason was calm now. Without realizing it, he loosened his grip on the branch and was now floating toward the drop. He closed his eyes, but Gabriel told him it would be more exciting if he kept his eyes open.

"It's a magnificent drop, Jason. You don't want to miss out on any part of it."

Following Gabriel's advice, Jason opened his eyes just before the current pulled him over the edge. Great excitement flowed over him as he went down.

"Wow." he gasped, as he safely landed in the water below.

Jason looked up, wiping away the water that had splashed into his eyes, and saw his dad standing by the edge of the river, now clapping his hands with joy.

"Bravo! Bravo!" Dad yelled. He threw his inner tube back in the water and jumping in just in time to meet up with Jason.

They were both wearing big grins when they met up with each other. Dad ruffled Jason's wet hair and said, "I am so proud of you! It was great watching you come down that drop with your eyes wide open and a smile of excitement on your face!"

"It was fun, Dad!" Jason exclaimed.

About the minutes later, they reached the spot where they wanted to get out of the water, and helped each other get their inner tubes over to the edge of the river, onto dry land.

They walked back to their campsite, laughing all the way about their exciting ride on the river and that fabulous drop.

As they reached their destination, Jason turned to his dad. "Dad," he began, "it really is true that when you let go of fear and trust your higher self, life can be so joyous and so much fun."

Dad looked at his son and smiled. "You've got that right, pal, and don't you forget it!"

He held the branch tightly, trying to think of a way out. There was no way he was going down that drop.

After a few minutes, he heard his dad's voice yelling, "Jason! Come on!"

He looked down the river again and saw his dad standing knee deep along the edge of the river, holding the inner tube on his left arm. He was waving for Jason to come down.

"I'll wait right here, but hurry up!" Dad called.

Jason's grip on the branch tightened. "No!" he shouted back, shaking his head. "I'm afraid!"

"But Jason," Dad called again, "The drop is not as far down as it looks. It's not scary. Really!"

Jason wouldn't let go. All he could do was shake his head in refusal.

"Jason," Dad continued, "you know you are safe! Just let go of your fear and trust your higher self to take care of you. You'll be safe and it'll be fun!"

Jason tried to relax. He took a few deep breaths and closed his eyes, listening to peaceful sound of the water moving downstream.

Gabriel came to him then. "What are you waiting for, my brother?" he asked.

Jason was glad to hear Gabriel's loving voice. "It sure looks like a big drop," he said.

"That's only because you can't see the bottom from where you are," Gabriel assured him. "It's really not that far down. I'm not afraid."

Jason laughed. "Ha! That's easy for you to say! You're not in a body, and you can go anywhere you want! But I'm still in my body, and the body can sometimes get hurt."

Gabriel chuckled. "But Jason, you are safe in that inner tube. Dad is right about trusting your higher self. You are here to have fun! It is only your thoughts that make things look fearful. Let go of those ideas and let your higher self take care of you! You will be safe and you'll have lots of fun!"

Day 25 ~ Story 25

I Let Go
And Let My Father
Be My Guide

It was another beautiful weekend—perfect for camping. This time, Jason and his parents went to Zion National Park to spend the weekend. After they set up camp, Jason and his dad went to ride inner tubes down the river, while his mom relaxed under a shade tree with a good book.

Jason and his dad were having fun, laughing all the way down the river. Suddenly Dad noticed a drop in the river up ahead. "Follow me!" he shouted. "This is going to be fun!" Then he disappeared over the edge, into the foamy water below.

Jason was afraid. He quickly grabbed the branch of a nearby tree and stopped himself from going any further. He looked down the river past the drop, hoping to catch a glimpse of his dad, who was nowhere to be seen.

"What do you mean?" Jason asked.

"Well," Gabriel continued, "I could go into the future and see it according to the way things are going in your life now, but if you decide to change the direction of your life, it is possible that the time of your transition will change, too. It's really up to you."

Jason found this very comforting. He smiled and said sleepily, "You're always watching over me, aren't you?"

Gabriel responded warmly, "You can count on that, my brother."

As Jason drifted off to sleep, he asked, "Are we going out to play tonight?"

Gabriel softly replied, "I'll be waiting right here for you, Jason. See you in a little while."

the time, when you wake up, you don't remember."

Jason became excited about this. "But I do remember sometimes, Gabriel! Sometimes I wake up and remember being with you, and playing and having fun in places where it seems I have never been before. I always thought I was just dreaming, but there are times when it seems more than just a dream—it seems so real."

"It is real, my brother," Gabriel continued. "I always wait for you to come out and play with me, and we do have lots of fun."

Feeling a little sleepy now, Jason lay down on the bed. But before he went to sleep he had one more question. "Gabriel," he asked, "do you know when I will make my transition?"

That was the question Gabriel had been waiting for. He knew Jason would ask eventually, and he was ready to answer. "Yes, I do, but it's not certain."

being, which is spirit. As spirit, we can be anywhere at any time. The only thing that limits us is our awareness of the body."

While Jason understood what his brother Gabriel was saying, he was still confused. He liked his body, and now he was not sure how he was supposed to feel about it.

He expressed his confusion and Gabriel told him, "I didn't say you shouldn't like your body, Jason. The point is that you must realize that you are not your body—you are experiencing yourself as a body, but you are actually much greater than just a body."

As Jason began to understand this truth, he felt very powerful. His confusion began to disappear as Gabriel continued. "When you are in your true state as spirit, you realize you have the power to create everything you want, and the ability to go anywhere, any time you want. I am here with you because I choose to be. We had an agreement, remember?"

"Of course I remember!" Jason smiled at this thought. That was the greatest agreement he had ever made in his life!

He thought of another question, and asked Gabriel, "Did it hurt when you made your transition?"

"No," Gabriel told him. "I left my body right before it appeared to die. And I want you to know that everything you hear about pain and dying is not true. You don't have to feel any pain when the time comes to make your transition. All you really have to do is lay the body down and go on to wherever you wish."

"And this is true for everyone?" Jason quietly asked, already knowing the answer.

"Yes, for everyone," Gabriel replied. "We were all created as part of the universe and, in truth, we are all as great as the universe."

As Gabriel spoke, more questions popped into Jason's head. He asked, "If I am greater than the body, why can't I leave the body whenever I want to, instead of just when it is time to make the transition out of it forever?"

"Good question!" Gabriel exclaimed. "And the answer is—you can, and you do! Every night when your body is sleeping, your spirit leaves and goes many different places and experiences many different things. But most of

help him sleep now.

As he looked through his bookshelf trying to decide which book to read, Gabriel's voice entered his mind.

"What's going on, my brother? Why can't you sleep?"

Jason quietly replied, "I don't know, Gabriel. It's weird. It's the middle of the night, but I'm wide awake."

"Would you like to talk?" Gabriel asked him.

After a moment, Jason replied, "As a matter of fact, I would like to talk. I have some questions for you."

"All right," Gabriel said happily, "what's on your mind?" Gabriel loved being able to help Jason. He especially loved teaching him how powerful and wonderful he was.

"What happens when you die," Jason began, "and how is it that you can still be here with me in my mind?"

Gabriel chuckled. "Well, those are pretty intense questions popping into your head in the middle of the night. It's no wonder you couldn't sleep."

Jason did not want to joke around. He just wanted some answers. "Well?" he asked with a serious tone in his voice.

Gabriel could see Jason was in no mood to laugh, and he knew he needed to do something to lighten things up.

"I'll tell you—if you really want to know," he said gently to his brother.

"Tell me, Gabriel." Jason responded. "I do want to know."

"Okay," Gabriel began. "Do you remember the conversation we had with Dad last year when he told us we were here to help each other?"

Jason remembered. It was this conversation that had brought him closer than ever to Gabriel.

Gabriel continued, "It was then that Dad told us we can never die—and he was right. What happens when it appears that we die is that we simply lose our awareness of the body and we transition back to our original state of

Day 24 ~ Story 24

My Father Is Great
And So Am I

It was the middle of the night and, for the second time, Jason got up for a drink of water. When he returned to bed, he tossed and turned endlessly, and just could not sleep.

After about ten minutes, Jason decided to get up and read. Sometimes when he would read at bedtime, he would drift off to sleep. Maybe reading would

how long he and the wolf had been there together. By the time he began to wonder how long it had been, the wolf was gracefully walking away, into the woods.

As the wolf moved out of sight, the peace Jason had felt was being replaced by excitement over what had just happened. He had just been a few feet away from a live wolf!"

Jason heard his brother's joyous voice saying, "Doesn't it feel good to love nature?"

"Oh, yes!" Jason said.

Gabriel told him the wolf was feeling the same way. "He felt your love and trust, Jason, and that's why he remained calm."

Jason stood up, still holding the firewood he had collected earlier, and returned to the campsite. As he excitedly told his parents about his meeting with the wolf, his dad expressed some concern.

But Mom quickly said, "Honey, don't worry about it. Jason has so much love, nothing at all can hurt him. It's almost as if someone is watching over him."

Dad had to agree. "Well, it does seem that way, doesn't it?"

Jason smiled and quietly murmured, "Yes, Gabriel is here."

Not hearing Jason's comment, his parents laughed with the comfort of knowing their son was protected. Jason was equally comforted, knowing the same protection was available to his parents.

Jason dropped the firewood into the pit, to prepare for roasting marshmallows after dinner. That was one of his favorite things to do while camping, along with—of course—admiring the wildlife.

peace and quiet was now surrounding them both.

Jason had never before seen a live wolf. He slowly sat on a nearby rock and whispered to the wolf in true wonderment, "You are beautiful." As Jason watched, the wolf continued to stare. It was almost as if he was admiring Jason, too.

After a few moments, the wolf began moving toward Jason. As Jason watched the wolf getting closer to him, the fear he had successfully overcome earlier was calling again. But he chose to listen to Gabriel's voice instead.

"Trust nature, my beloved brother," he heard Gabriel's loving voice say. "This wolf is not here to hurt you."

The wolf moved closer, and Jason called upon that trust. Smiling, he looked again into the wolf's eyes. Peace flowed freely now, as the connection between these two living creatures was felt by each of them.

Jason had lost all sense of time. He had no idea

Jason felt a great sense of peace flow over him as he heard Gabriel respond, "Yes, I am here, and we are not lost!"

He smiled. "Then why," he asked, "doesn't any of this look familiar?"

"You've walked over a small hill which is blocking your view of the campsite," Gabriel explained. "If you walk to the right, you'll be back in no time."

Jason looked to the right and noticed the hill Gabriel had spoken of. He began walking toward it, but suddenly Gabriel told him, "Hold it, Jason— don't move. Stay right where you are."

Confused, Jason asked, "What do you mean? I've collected all the wood I need, and I'm hungry!"

"Jason," Gabriel continued gently, "I want you to stand there and remain calm. Remember—I am with you, and you can trust me."

Jason could sense there was something going on that he was not aware of. That old feeling of fear began creeping up, but Jason reminded himself that he trusted Gabriel and was totally safe with him there.

He heard some rustling in the woods behind him, and Gabriel calmly told him, "There is a wolf behind you. If you become afraid and run away, the wolf will come after you, thinking that you are playing with him. But if you turn around and look at the wolf, admiring his beauty, he will feel your calmness, and will remain calm, too."

Jason did not move. Fear was calling to him, but he trusted Gabriel and knew that what he was saying was true. He called upon that trust to give him the strength to do what was necessary.

Gabriel was pleased at Jason's calmness, and he continued. "Now is the time for you to learn to trust that nature created this wolf in total peace, and it is only your thoughts of fear about him that would cause him to become fearful and vicious."

Jason took a deep breath and turned around. The sight that met his eyes was one of great wonder. About twenty feet into the woods behind him stood a gray wolf, his fur shining with the reflection of the setting sun. Jason could feel gooseflesh covering his body as the wolf's eyes met his. It seemed as if all the sounds of the forest had suddenly come to a halt. A great sense of wilderness and all its beauty and life. As late afternoon arrived, the family began settling down at their campsite for the evening.

Mom was preparing the evening meal, and asked Jason to gather some wood to build a fire for roasting marshmallows after dinner. This was one of Jason's favorite things to do! He gladly walked into the woods, carefully choosing, as his father had taught him, only the pieces of wood that he knew would be good for burning.

Jason walked and walked until he had enough wood for a small fire, and then decided to head back to the campsite. Looking up, he realized he was not sure which way to go. He had wandered too far, and now he was lost.

As fear began to grip him, he took a few deep breaths to relax. He had learned well not to allow fear to take over his mind, so he looked around at the peaceful sights and sounds of the forest and called to Gabriel.

Day 23 ~ Story 23

I Trust My Father

The summer weather had arrived! Jason always looked forward to this time of year because his parents liked to take him camping on the weekends. They had decided their first camping trip of the year would be to Yellowstone National Park.

Jason and his parents had a beautiful day hiking in the park, enjoying the

"There is a part of you, beyond your body, that knows everything. It is what connects us to each other and to all the universe. This higher self loves you more than you love yourself! It was this Universal Love that guided me to walk, this way, to be there for you when you were wishing for a friend."

Jack looked at Jason thoughtfully. He felt a sense of peace come over him as he listened to what Jason was saying. And something told him—his higher self, maybe—that what Jason was saying was the truth.

Jason continued, "If you are ever tempted to put yourself in that kind of situation again, please remember this experience and make a better decision."

"You bet I will." Jack laughed,

The boys gave each other a high-five and agreed to watch out for each other from that time on. Then they continued their walk home, feeling joyous from the love of the universe that surrounded them both.

As Jason opened his mind to repeat Gabriel's words, he heard himself saying calmly to the man, "Listen, I know your name is Raul, and you live at 232 Valley View, Apartment #62. Your probation officer is Mr. Thompson."

The man was shocked at what this young boy was telling him. This boy seemed to know everything about him!

Jason could feel the man's grip loosening on his arm, and at that moment he knew he had accomplished his goal.

"Would you like me to say more," he asked the man, his voice steady and confident, "or are you going to get your hands off both of us and leave us alone?"

Still in shock, with his jaw hanging open in amazement, the man dropped Jason's arm and began backing away from him. He turned and pointed at Jack, clenching his teeth.

"You and your friend stay away from me," he said harshly. "I don't want to talk to you anymore."

As Jack and Jason watched, the man turned away and quickly ran across the street and around the corner, out of sight. Jack turned to Jason with a look of relief on his face.

"Wow!" he said, "How did you know all that about him?"

Never mind about that," Jason replied. "Let's get out of here before he decides to come back. I'm heading home. Are you?"

"Uh-huh," Jack replied, still a bit surprised at what just happened.

As the two boys walked home together, Jason asked, "By the way Jack, why do you hang around with guys who use cigarettes?"

With his head hung low, slightly, embarrassed, Jack quietly replied, "I'm not going to talk to him anymore. You know, Jason."

Jack paused for a moment, feeling as if a heavy weight had been lifted from his shoulders. He looked at Jason and told him, "Jason, you were really a good friend back there. Thanks, buddy."

Jason smiled at Jack. "I want you to know something," he answered.

Jason called upon his inner strength and suddenly felt very brave. He walked directly over to his friend and said, "Hi, Jack! What's going on?"

The man was startled by Jason's sudden arrival, and he stepped back.

Jack turned to Jason with a frightened look and tears in his eyes and replied, "Oh, nothing, Jason, nothing at all. Don't worry about it."

The man chuckled and moved closer to Jack, putting his arm around the boy's shoulder. "Yeah," he said in a stern voice, "do like your friend says, and don't worry about it, kid. Just keep walking."

Jason did not move. "I'm not going anywhere until I find out what's going on."

The man slowly removed his arm from around Jack's shoulder. He walked over to where Jason was standing and stared down at him with a very mean look on his face. "If you know what's good for you, kid, you'll keep walking, like I said."

At that moment, Jason felt fear beginning to creep into his mind. Then he remembered that Gabriel was with him. As the thought of his brother replaced his thoughts of fear, he heard Gabriel say, "Stay calm, my brother. He cannot hurt you. I am here."

This gave Jason the strength he needed to continue. He took a step closer to the man and looked into his eyes. "Leave my friend alone," he told the man in a voice so brave and strong he didn't recognize himself, "or I am going to call the police."

The man was shocked. He had never expected any kid to stand up to him so bravely. He stepped back and looked at Jason with a hint of confusion in his eyes. His voice softened a bit as he said, "Kid, this doesn't concern you. Just go away."

"You're wrong about that," he told the man. "It does concern me, and I'm not going anywhere without Jack."

Suddenly the man became angry. He grabbed Jason's arm, but by this time Jason felt so strong that nothing could frighten him. He continued to hear Gabriel's voice.

"Jason, now I want you to repeat exactly what I tell you." Gabriel said.

Let's take the long way home today," Gabriel suggested. "We've got plenty of time."

Jason agreed it would be fun to go a different way for a change. He turned around and walked back toward the street that would lead him to the long way home.

As Jason approached the corner where he needed to turn, Gabriel told him to stop.

"Listen to me, Jason," Gabriel began. "When you reach the corner, you will see a big man trying to convince your friend Jack to buy some drugs. Don't get excited. Just keep your cool

and go over and be with Jack. He is wishing he had a friend right now."

Jason hesitated for a moment. "But it sounds dangerous, Gabriel."

"It's not dangerous," Gabriel replied. "If you listen to me and do exactly what I tell you, everything will be cool."

Jason was unsure exactly what he was supposed to do, but he trusted Gabriel, and he knew that with Gabriel's help he would do the right thing. He was excited by what was about to happen, but he felt very safe.

As Jason turned the corner, he saw Jack leaning up against a tree, talking to the man Gabriel had described earlier.

Day 22 ~ Story 22

My Father Loves Me
More Than I Love Myself

One day there was a special teacher's meeting at school, so classes were dismissed early. As Jason walked home along his usual route, Gabriel asked him, "Jason, do you want to do something different today, and have some fun?"

Jason replied, "Sure. What is it?"

Dad had just taken the last bite of an apple and said, "I'm ready, pal!" He stood up and walked over to his wife. Kissing her, he said, "Thanks, honey. That was a great lunch. How about joining us at the lake? Our son is quite a fisherman."

Jason added, "Yeah, Mom, it's so much fun!"

Jason's mother agreed to join them, and felt a warm love surrounding her as she walked to the lake with her family.

Gabriel told Jason there were lots of fish on the other side of the lake, so the three of them caught and released dozens of fish before the day was over. It was the best fishing they had done in their lives.

When it was time to go home, the three of them packed all the food and fishing gear and headed toward the car. Jason felt a strong love flowing through him, and he said to his parents, "I really love these family outings when all four of us spend the day together having so much fun!"

His mom giggled. "What do you mean, 'the four of us'? Do you have a mouse in your pocket?"

Jason laughed and replied, "Oh, I mean the three of us."

His parents smiled at each other, and shrugged.

As they reached the car, Jason heard Gabriel say, "Watch it, my brother—you almost blew our cover!"

Jason just grinned, thankful for his brother's guidance and the unconditional love that surrounded him.

Jason grinned back. "Yeah, Dad! Can I unhook him?"

"Sure thing." Dad replied, and he watched his son gently unhook the fish as he had shown him earlier.

When Jason had the hook safely out of fish's mouth, he handed the fish to his father. "You do it this time," he said.

Dad took the bass and tossed it gently back into the water.

Mom's voice suddenly called to them, "Lunch is ready! Come on, guys!"

Jason looked at his dad and said, "Oh good, I'm starving! Can we fish some more after lunch?"

"You bet." Dad replied, and walked with his son over to where Mom had prepared a wonderful lunch of sandwiches, salads and fruit.

After gobbling down a healthy serving of all the food his mom had prepared, Jason stood up and said, "Thanks, Mom. That was delicious." Then he turned to his dad and asked, "Are you ready for more fishing?"

"Promised?" Dad asked with confusion in his voice. "Promised who?"

Jason did not know what to say. "I can't explain right now, Dad, but I'm telling you, the fish has to go back."

Dad could see, by the concern in his son's face, that he was serious. "All right, then. It's your fish. If you want to release it, we'll release it."

Jason breathed a sigh of relief. "Great!" he exclaimed, and he knelt down to help his dad gently unhook the fish.

As Dad watched his son toss the fish back into the lake, he shook his head. "Jason," he began, "let me ask you something. If we're going to throw the fish back in the lake, why are we fishing in the first place?"

Jason thought for a moment. "Well, Dad, it's not really about catching fish—it's about being with you."

Dad was caught off guard. He placed his hands on Jason's shoulders and looked into his son's eyes. "What—what did you say?"

Jason repeated himself. "It's just about being with you, Dad. I love when we do fun things together. Isn't that really why we're doing this? To have fun together?"

At that moment, Dad felt a deep, unconditional love for his son. He put his arms around Jason and they hugged each other for a long time. Suddenly, Dad stepped back, looked at Jason, and whispered, "Let's go catch some more fish!"

Dad's pole was still in the sand, untouched, where he had left it. He reeled in the line and discovered it was still baited. There had not even been a nibble. He helped re-bait Jason's line, and it was not long after they cast their lines when Dad felt a tug. "It's a bite, Jason—I've got one!" he exclaimed as he reeled it in.

Jason dropped his pole and excitedly ran to his father's side. He watched as another big bass was reeled in. It was not quite as big as Jason's,

but it was big enough. They watched the fish flopping around on the sand for a few moments, and then looked at each other.

Dad grinned and said, "What do you say we throw him back?"

a man. He followed, as Jason had requested, and asked, "Where are we going?"

Jason said, "I know where there are some fish just waiting to be caught."

His dad was amused and very curious, so he followed. Just before they reached the tree, Jason told his dad about the hole in the lake bed.

"Sounds good to me." Dad said.

He and Jason baited their lines, and within a few seconds of casting, Jason had a bite!

He began to reel it in, but the fish was too strong and the line would not move.

Dad quickly and firmly stuck his pole in the sand and rushed over to Jason's side. He positioned himself behind Jason, with one hand on the pole and the other helping Jason turn the reel.

"I think you got a big one!" Dad shouted.

"Don't let him get away, Dad!" Jason screamed in delight.

The sounds of their excitement filled the park, and Mom came running over to see what was going on. For the next ten minutes, Mom cheered for her husband and son, until they finally reeled in the fish—the largest bass they had ever seen!

As Jason sct down the pole and they all watched their prize fish flopping on the shore, Dad exclaimed, "What a magnificent catch! We'll clean it up and cook it for dinner tomorrow!"

"Sounds good to me." said Mom, and she walked back over to the picnic area to finish preparing lunch.

Jason was about to agree until he remembered his promise to Gabriel. "No, Dad, we can't do that," he said. "We have to put the fish back."

Dad looked at his son, and his smile faded. "What do you mean, put it back? This is going to make us a great dinner!"

"But, Dad," Jason continued, "I promised to put it back."

"Just give me a minute, Dad," Jason replied. He sat beneath the tree and quietly called Gabriel.

"Yes, my loving brother," Gabriel responded. "What do you need?"

"Gabriel," Jason began, "I'd really like to catch some fish."

Gabriel laughed. "But why?"

Jason, who thought that the answer was obvious, responded, "Well, because it's fun, that's why!"

"Are you going to eat the fish?" Gabriel asked.

Jason thought about it for a moment and said, "Well, no, not really. I just want to catch them."

"Okay, so you want to catch them," Gabriel said. "Then what are you planning to do with them after you catch them?"

"Well," Jason replied, "I guess I'll throw them back into the lake."

Gabriel was pleased to hear this. "In that case, do you see that weeping willow tree about one hundred feet to the right of you?"

"Yes, Gabriel, I see it." Jason replied.

"Well, just before you reach the tree, there is a hole in the side of the lake bed where three large, hungry fish are looking for some food. Two of these fish are about to lay eggs, so it's important that you release them. Do you promise to release them?" Gabriel asked Jason.

"Of course." Jason replied, and ran back over to the shore where his dad was waiting.

"Come on, Dad, follow me!" he said, and took his dad's hand to lead him to the place where Gabriel told him they would find the fish.

His father was very surprised, because this was the first time he had even seen Jason take charge. It made him feel good to see his son behaving like

Day 21 ~ Story 21

My Father Loves Me Unconditionally

It was a beautiful day at the park. Mom was preparing lunch in the picnic area while Jason and his dad fished in the lake. They had been casting from the shore for over an hour without a bite.

Dad turned to Jason and jokingly said, "Jason, either this lake doesn't have any fish, or you and I are poor fishermen!"

They both laughed, and Jason replied, "Dad, I think we need help."

Dad responded with a chuckle, "You're right—we need all the help we can get."

But Jason was serious. "I'll be right back," he said, and slowly backed away from the shore toward a nearby tree.

"Where are you going?" Dad called.

Jason smiled and gently laughed. "I know what you mean. I felt the same way a few minutes ago when I was walking past the park. That was until I realized that there really is no fear."

Jenny slowed down a bit, obviously comforted that her friend was there. "There is no fear?" she asked. "What do you mean, Jason?"

Jason continued. "We put fear into our own minds by thinking fearful thoughts. We make it up! It doesn't really exist at all, Jenny."

"But it really seemed as if someone was following me!" she replied.

"I know," Jason said, "but turn around and look. Do you see anyone there?"

Jenny turned around. The street was quiet—they were the only people there. She looked at Jason and smiled, saying, "No, I guess not."

They both laughed for a few moments as Jenny realized the truth in Jason's words. Then she asked, "Jason, would you mind walking me home?"

Jason looked at her, and suddenly he felt very brave and grown up. "Of course not. I'd love to. Come on, let's go."

As the two friends walked and laughed together on that moonless night, Jason was thankful to know that he need never be afraid again.

Unfortunately, Jenny does not yet understand that fear doesn't exist. She is very afraid right now, as you were before, and she could really use your support."

By this time, Jason was feeling so full of love and peace that he had no trouble walking back past the park, to where he could find Jenny. He knew the turmoil that fear could bring to one's mind, and he didn't want Jenny feeling that way—not even for a second.

He ran back toward school and, within a minute, he saw Jenny. She was walking quickly, glancing over her shoulder with every other step. He slowed down as he approached her.

"Hi, Jenny! What's up?"

Her face was frozen with fear. "Jason, I'm so scared. I think someone is following me!"

shadowy figure hiding behind a tree.

Just as he was about to scream and run away, he remembered what Gabriel had said to him many times: "Only love is real, Jason—nothing else exists. Fear and anything that comes from fear is not real—it is only an illusion, so don't buy into it."

He heard those words, "Don't but into it." in his head, and they gave him the strength he needed.

At that moment, Jason stopped walking. He stood on the sidewalk and very calmly turned around to look into the darkness of the park. Then he said out loud to himself, "I am not afraid. There is nothing to be afraid of. I refuse to buy into this illusion of fear."

Jason looked all around him. He realized that no one was following him, and the footsteps he heard were his own, echoing off the sidewalk. He understood now that the rustling he heard in the bushes was caused by the breeze, which he now could feel gently blowing through his hair.

He noticed that the shadowy figure behind the tree was nothing more than the shadow of the tree itself, dancing in the glare of a street light. As Jason stood there, silent now, he closed his eyes and felt a sense of peace and quiet come over him.

Suddenly, Gabriel's voice seemed to echo in his head. "Jason! You can finally hear me! I am so glad you chose to let go of that fear. There is no one in this park except you, me, and one homeless person who is peacefully sleeping under a tree on the other side of the park."

Jason had to laugh. The thoughts that had terrified him just moments before, now seemed ridiculous. "Wow," he said. "I really got myself worked up over nothing, didn't I?"

Gabriel responded, "The important thing is that you brought yourself out of that fear almost as quickly as you got into it. Bravo, my brother!"

Jason smiled. Gabriel always knew how to bring a smile to his face.

Gabriel continued. "Now there is someone who needs your help, Jason. If you walk back the way you came, you will see your classmate, Jenny, is also walking home along this path.

school, and as he passed it now, he was afraid. There were no baseball games being played, so the lights were off. It was very dark.

Suddenly, Jason heard a rustling noise that seemed to be coming from the bushes near the children's play area. He found himself thinking about all the stories he had heard from other kids—stories about homeless people wandering around in the dark, stealing from others, and mean people kidnapping children and hurting them. These thoughts terrified him, and he began to walk faster.

He thought he heard footsteps behind him, and his fear grew. He quickly turned around, but no one was there.

He walked even faster now, and caught a glimpse of what he thought was a

Day 20 ~ Story 20

Only Love Exists–
Fear Is an Illusion

It was a moonless night, and Jason was walking home from school. Although he had stayed after school to watch a special movie, he did not go home when the movie was over. He had stayed even longer to talk with some of his friends, and now he had to walk home in the dark.

There was a baseball park beside the path between Jason's home and his

your things, that's his problem, and there is nothing for you to feel guilty about. It's important that you always be true to yourself and do what you know is right for you."

Gabriel's explanation made sense to Jason. He started feeling good about himself again, and was glad that he had asked Jim to respect his stuff. But he was still concerned about one thing, and asked Gabriel, "Are you sure Jim will be back?"

Gabriel asked gently, "Have I ever steered you wrong?"

Jason laughed. "No, Gabriel. Never."

Jason's headache was gone now, and his stomach was growling with hunger. He raced downstairs to the kitchen. His parents were still eating breakfast, and when they saw Jason they put down their forks.

Mom jumped up from her chair and walked over to him. "How are you feeling, honey?" she asked.

Jason looked up at her and said, "Much better, Mom. The only thing I need now, besides a stack of those pancakes, is a hug from both of you."

As Jason put his arms around his mom, Dad stood up from his chair, walked over to his wife and son and joined their hugging. After they all expressed their love for each other, Jason exclaimed, "Let's eat!"

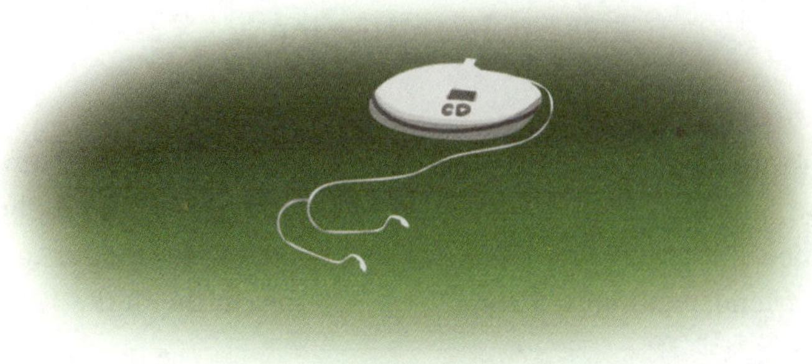

"Not really," Jason said. "I have a stomachache. I think I'll go lie down for a while."

Dad gave Jason a hug. "Okay, pal. Let me know if I can get you anything."

"Thanks, Dad," Jason said as he turned to go to his room.

Jason headed upstairs. He was not feeling very good about himself, and he was sad that he may have lost his friend Jim. He entered his room and closed the door softly behind him.

As the door closed, he could faintly hear his brother Gabriel's voice. He knew it was Gabriel, but it sounded so far away that he could not understand what his brother was saying. Jason knew it was the turmoil in his mind that was preventing him from hearing Gabriel, and that he was going to have to calm down and ask peace to enter his mind.

He lay down on his bed and began to breathe deeply. With every breath, he was released his thoughts of shame, guilt and sadness, and replacing them with the idea of light and love filling his entire mind and body.

It worked. Jason began to feel a sense of peace flowing over him, and he could clearly hear Gabriel's concerned voice.

"Jason, what's going on? Why are you upset?"

"I was feeling bad about being mean to Jim."

"My brother, you were not mean," Gabriel said quietly. "Jim has a habit of breaking all of his games and toys, but you take care of yours. There was nothing wrong with you asking him to respect your stuff. You did the right thing."

"But I feel bad," Jason answered. "I like Jim, and he told me he doesn't want to come over anymore because I wouldn't let him play with my stuff."

"That's okay. He'll change his mind," Gabriel assured Jason. "Have you forgotten that you are a very loving person? You love everybody! And you are also very lovable—everyone loves you, because you are always kind and gentle."

"But," Gabriel added, "don't buy into other people's habits and problems. If Jim likes to destroy his own things and you do not allow him to destroy

Jason started feeling anger coming over him. He turned to his friend and said, "Jim, I don't want you to touch the CD player anymore. That is the third CD you have ruined tonight! Please don't touch the CD player anymore."

Jim lowered his head and walked to the other side of the room with a hurt look on his face.

Tom and Jason looked at each other and shrugged. Then Jason moved the CD player and some of his important games from the floor to the dresser, so they would not get ruined.

After a few minutes, the incident was forgotten and the boys were all playing happily together again.

The next morning, Jim and Tom's parents arrived to take the boys home. Tom said good-bye and thanked Jason for having him over. "See you at school on Monday!" he called as he ran toward the street, waving to his mom who was waiting in the car.

Jim's dad arrived shortly after Tom left. As he heard the horn beeping from the driveway, Jim opened the front door and turned to Jason. "I'm not coming over to your house anymore," he said. "You're too stingy with your games and stuff. You won't even let your friends play with them!" Not waiting for Jason to respond, Jim ran to his dad, calling, "Hi, Dad!"

Jason felt shocked and hurt. Even though he believed that Jim's statement was untrue, he felt a sense of shame and blame coming over him. After all, he wanted his friends to have fun when they came to his house.

As Jason closed the front door, he heard his dad calling from the kitchen. "Breakfast is almost ready! Come and eat, Jason!"

He was feeling sick to his stomach, and his head was throbbing. The thought of food made him want to throw up. He walked into the kitchen and said, "Dad, I'm not really hungry right now."

Knowing that his dad would insist that he eat breakfast, he quickly added, "I'll eat in a little while, okay?"

His dad looked at him with concern. He knelt down and touched Jason's forehead. "You look pale, buddy. Are you feeling okay?"

Day 19 ~ Story 19

I Am Loving and Lovable

It was Saturday night, and Jason was having a sleepover at his house with his two friends, Tom and Jim. The boys were having a great time listening to music, telling jokes, and laughing together. Jim had been acting a bit crazy, and for the third time that evening he kicked the compact disc player and scratched one of Jason's CD's.

ready to accept it.

His mom stood there silently, not knowing what to expect.

Suddenly, Dad smiled and threw his arms around his son. "Oh, Jason, you are so magnificent! I really love you! Thank you for telling me the truth. I wish your brother could be here to see this—he would be so proud of you!"

Jason smiled, and muttered under his breath, "He'd better be."

Jason's mom was relieved at how the situation had turned out. She hugged Jason too, and whispered in his ear, "You're an amazing kid!"

Jason spent the next two hours completing his homework. When he finished, he felt free and very peaceful. Then he ran downstairs, just in time to greet his cousins at the door. They played games and had fun all night long, and Jason never thought about his school work—not even once.

As Jason lay down to sleep that night, Gabriel asked him, "So, how are you feeling, my brother?"

Jason smiled very peacefully. "I am feeling so lucky to have you! Everything is wonderful! I had so much fun tonight, and I couldn't have done it without you. Thank you, Gabriel—I love you."

The last thing Jason heard before drifting off to sleep that night was Gabriel's soft voice saying, "I love you, too."

Gabriel tried to reason with Jason. "Brother," he said softly, "you can't have fun when you are in turmoil deep inside. You must choose peace—only peace. Only by choosing peace will you experience joy, fun and laughter. Don't try to put joy and fun on top of turmoil and worry—it will not work."

Jason sat at his computer, thinking about what Gabriel was saying. It all made perfect sense, and he knew it was true. Of course he wanted only peace, but after thinking about the party tonight, he just didn't feel like doing homework.

As Jason thought about what to do, Gabriel continued. "Also, brother, remember who we are. Our word is very powerful—we must speak only truth. You forgot about that when you lied and told Dad you didn't have any homework to do, and you are feeling uncomfortable about it now.

It is against your true nature to lie. Deep down inside, you know this."

Gabriel's voice trailed off as Jason heard his dad calling him to come downstairs. He headed to the living room, knowing he had to make things right. He had to tell his dad the truth.

"Uh, Dad—?" he began.

But his dad interrupted him. "Oh, Jason—thanks for coming down. I'm so glad you don't have any homework—we could really use your help! Before you start on getting your games set up, would you mind helping your mom and me get these decorations finished?"

Jason heard Gabriel's soft voice. "Truth, my brother. Always tell the truth. You do not have to lie."

Gabriel's support gave Jason the strength he needed at that moment. He looked into his father's eyes and said, "Dad, I have something to tell you."

Dad knelt down to Jason's level and said, "What is it, Jason?"

Jason began, "I'm sorry, Dad. I lied to you. I do have homework tonight— lots of it, and I'd like to get it done before the party, so I can be at peace about it, and really have fun."

Dad quietly looked at Jason for a moment.

Jason wasn't sure what his dad was going to do, but whatever it was, he was

"Great!" Jason said. "Are my cousins coming, too?"

His dad grinned and replied, "Of course!"

"Alright!" Jason shouted. "I'd better get my computer ready and set up some games for us to play!"

As he ran toward his bedroom, his dad called after him, "Jason, wait!"

Jason stopped and turned around. "Yes, Dad?"

"Do you have any homework tonight, son?"

Jason quickly responded, "No, nothing."

Dad smiled. "Okay then," he said. "Go ahead and get ready to have some fun!"

As Jason headed up to his room, there was a very uncomfortable feeling in the pit of his stomach. He had lied to his dad—he did have homework that night.

Climbing the stairs, he heard Gabriel's voice saying, "Jason! Why did you lie?"

Jason was embarrassed, and didn't know how to answer. He was uncomfortable enough in knowing he had lied to his dad, but he felt even worse now that Gabriel knew.

In response to Jason's thoughts, Gabriel said, "I am part of you, my brother! I know everything about you."

Jason reached his room, closed the door and quietly responded, "I don't know why I lied. I just didn't want to have to worry about my homework right now."

Gabriel gently told his brother, "Jason, you know your school work is very important. If you don't get your homework done, you will worry about it all evening and you won't be able to have any fun."

"No I won't," Jason quickly responded. Then he sat on his bed with his head hung low. "I'll—I'll be fine." He stood up and walked over to start up his computer.

Day 18 ~ Story 18

I Choose Only Peace

One afternoon as Jason arrived home from school, he found his parents busy decorating the house with balloons and party favors.

Jason walked over to his father and gave him a hug. "Hi, Dad, what's going on?" he asked.

Dad hugged Jason back. "Today is our wedding anniversary," he said. "Your mom and I have invited our friends and family over to celebrate. It's going to be a big night!"

replied. "The worrying is exactly what is causing your problem."

"But if I don't worry, how can I trust that I will study hard and get A's?" Jason asked.

Gabriel answered him. "The simple solution is to trust your higher self. Remember, your body is not who you are. The part of you that is one with all the universe is who you really are! When you trust your higher self, you open your mind to joy and peace about things like studying, and you open yourself to receiving miracles, like getting all A's on your tests. When you are open to receive miracles and know that you deserve them, they will be given to you. Miracles are always there, just waiting for your acceptance."

Jason thought about what Gabriel was saying. He did not understand what caused him to worry so much, but he knew he did not want to feel the turmoil of worrying anymore.

He was glad Gabriel reminded him that he was not just a helpless body. He knew he was much more than that! He had seen before what the power of his mind could create, and he decided right then to trust his higher self, and to be open to receive all the miracles that were waiting for his acceptance. He knew he deserved them.

Very much at peace now, Jason decided he had studied enough for the day and would continue tomorrow with a clear mind. He crawled under his covers. After saying a loving good-night to Gabriel, he quickly drifted into a long and restful sleep.

A few days later, the tests were over and the results were in. Jason was not surprised to discover that he had gotten A's on every one of his tests. He was very happy about this, and so were his mom and dad.

He knew he deserved the A's, and that as long as he was open to receive miracles, every wonderful thing would be given to him.

helplessness and loss of control suddenly came over him. He began to cry, and he cried until he was too tired to cry anymore. Feeling worn out, he quietly lay on his bed and closed his eyes, trying to be at peace.

"I haven't thought about Gabriel for a while," he suddenly realized. "I miss him."

As if responding to his thought, Gabriel's said, "It's about time, my brother! I thought you had

forgotten about me!"

"Gabriel!" Jason replied. "Where have you been? I haven't heard your voice for a long time!"

"I've been here, but you haven't thought about me," Gabriel said. "You've been busy worrying about your tests. You know, Jason, whenever you worry, you close the door on me. I cannot come in and talk to you, because you can't hear me. All you can hear are the voices of your worrying.

Jason just lay there quietly for a few moments. The sound of Gabriel's voice had brought the feeling of peace he was looking for.

"You can hear me now because when you cried, you cleared your mind of all the worrying, and realized you wished to be at peace," Gabriel added. "This opened your mind to be able to receive my help."

Although Jason was calm now, he still thought about his tests. "I was worrying about my grades on my final tests, and I don't really know what to do about it," he said.

"What you do about it my beloved brother, is, stop worrying!" Gabriel

Day 17 ~ Story 17

I Am Open To Receive Miracles

It was getting close to the end of the school semester, and Jason was preparing for his final tests. Although he spent a lot of time studying, he was worried about the results. He wanted to get all A's, but didn't think it would be possible because some of the work was just too hard to understand.

Jason had been spending so much time thinking about the tests, he hadn't talked with or even thought about Gabriel for what seemed like a very long time. Then, one evening as he was in his bedroom studying, a sense of

He was ready to say something very harsh to Richie, but he heard Gabriel's voice.

"Jason, you don't have to be upset," Gabriel said. "Richie will learn his lesson—somehow, some way. Your job is simply to make the right decision for yourself. You don't have to hang around with him or accept his invitation. What he does, need not have any effect on you."

Jason understood. "Thanks for the invitation, but I'm not interested in going to a party where people get going to a party like this way. That's not what being cool is all about."

By this time, Jason and Tom had finished their lunch, so they stood up, said good-bye to Richie, and headed back to their classroom. Tom had not said a word while the two were talking, but now he looked at Jason with a big grin on his face. Nudging him with an elbow, Tom said, "Wow! You handled that great! You really are the coolest!"

Jason laughed and replied, "Yeah, it was easy!" and he quietly thanked Gabriel for his guidance.

Gabriel responded, "My brother, as long as I am with you, you will not get into trouble, because I will always guide you to the direction of peace. Thank you for being open to my guidance. I love you."

Jason quietly replied, "I love you, too."

big brother is having a party at our house. He told me I could invite some of my cool friends. Would you like to come?"

Jason grinned. He was about to accept the invitation when he heard Gabriel's voice saying, "Pause for a moment before you react, my brother. Find out what kind of party it is going to be, first."

Jason paused, and then asked, "What kind of party is it going to be?"

"Oh, you know," Richie replied. "For cool people. My brother has a lot of cool friends who will give us alcohol to drink, and cigarettes to smoke, and maybe even some other stuff. We'll all have a great time!"

Jason was shocked. "You guys do things not supposed to do?"

Richie chuckled. "Well, what else would cool people do?" he asked. That's why we're cool, isn't it?"

Jason became very quiet. He remembered what his parents always told him about cigarettes and alcohol. He knew that cigarettes and alcohol destroy the brain and body, and that people who get drunk and use cigarettes always end up ruining their lives and being very unhappy.

Day 16 ~ Story 16

I Pause Before I React

It was lunchtime on a beautiful sunny day. Jason was eating lunch on the grass in the schoolyard with his good friend Tom. As they ate their sandwiches, a boy named Richie, from another class, walked up to him and said, "Hey Jason, you're a pretty cool guy."

Jason looked up at Richie and smiled. "Thanks." he said.

Richie sat down next to Jason. They talked for a few minutes about school activities while Tom quietly sat and listened.

"You know, Jason," Richie said, "my parents are going out of town and my

Jason turned the box upside-down, but couldn't find any batteries. He looked around outside of the box, but still no batteries. He really wanted to play with the robot right away, but since he couldn't, he turned to open some more presents instead.

As Jason unwrapped his other gifts, he was excited to find so many wonderful things—nice clothes, new games and books, and a lot of fun toys—some of which needed batteries. But again, no batteries were included with the gifts.

Jason continued, picking up the present Grandma Betty had brought that morning, and unwrapping it. "Wow!" he yelled. "Thanks, Grandma Betty, this is just what I need! Batteries!"! He now had all the batteries he would need for his robot and the other toys, too—and he would even have some left over.

As Jason laughed happily, Grandma Betty chuckled and explained, "I knew that everyone who bought battery-operated toys for you would forget the batteries, so it was my job to supply them."

Jason jumped up and gave his grandma a big hug. He realized that it was a good thing that he had been patient about waiting for Christmas Day to open his presents. If he had opened them any sooner, he would have been very disappointed to find such wonderful toys that he could not play with because he had no batteries.

Because he was patient, he had avoided the disappointment. Instead, he had enjoyed a wonderful, joyous Christmas with his family.

evening he looked at that box, wondering what was in it. He wished he could open it, but his parents had told him he would have to wait until Christmas Day.

He begged and pleaded with them to let him open it sooner, but it was no use. They told him to be patient, and they were firm about their decision. He would have to wait.

Finally Christmas morning arrived. Many of Jason's relatives came over to exchange gifts. Even Grandma Betty had traveled all the way from Australia to be with the family for Christmas.

Grandma Betty had brought many gifts, and among them Jason saw a small, beautifully wrapped box with his name on it.

When the time came to open gifts, Jason grabbed the big box he had been eyeing all week, and tore at the wrapping paper. As he opened the box, what he saw brought a big grin to his face. Inside was a remote-control-operated robot! He had seen it in the store a few months ago, and had wished he could have it.

"Thanks, Mom! Thanks, Dad!" Jason shouted as he searched the box for batteries to get the robot moving.

Day 15 ~ Story 15

I Am Patient

Christmas would be here in a few days, and it was a happy time for everyone. Gifts were being exchanged and everyone was joyous, laughing all the time.

At Jason's house there was a huge box under the Christmas tree with his name on it. He was so anxious to open that box! Every morning and every

Ashley looked up at Jason, her eyes wide in surprise. "Really?" she asked.

"Yes—really," Jason said with a grin.

Seeing Jason's grin, Ashley couldn't help but grin back. "You know, Jason, I don't really think you're crazy for talking to your invisible someone. Actually I think you are very wise, because everything you do turns out to be wonderful. I really respect you—you're a great guy!"

Suddenly Jason felt that familiar, warm sense of joy and peace surrounding him. He had always liked Ashley, even more than he liked Susie, but had never thought he could be friends with her. He had always thought Ashley was a snob. But now, for the first time, he saw that she was a very gentle and loving person. He squeezed her hand tightly.

Ashley's eyes sparkled with a special light of joy. "I knew you were going to be my partner, even though we weren't lined up together." she said.

Jason laughed and asked, "How did you know?"

"I just knew." she answered, and gave his hand a squeeze back.

As the two new friends began their project together, Jason looked up toward Mrs. Johnson and quietly thanked his angel for working through her to do what was best for him.

Jason was not amused. He placed a hand over his mouth, as if yawning, and whispered to Gabriel, "What do you mean, 'what's best for me'? Having Susie as a partner would have been what's best for me."

"Have patience, my brother," Gabriel said. "Your angel knows what brings you the most joy and peace."

Jason knew that Gabriel was always right, so what could he do? Though it wasn't easy at first, he let go of the need to have Susie as a partner. He watched sadly as she was paired up with Nick and they crossed the room to begin their project.

He counted down the line of girls, to see who would be his partner. When he realized it would be Ashley, once again he couldn't believe his eyes. He and Ashley had argued last week, and Jason had decided not to talk to her anymore.

Too soon, both he and Ashley got to the front of their lines, and he slowly walked over to become her partner. With a look of disappointment she joined him, and they crossed the room together.

As they sat down to organize their project materials, Jason tried to think of something to say to Ashley, but he was very uncomfortable, and couldn't speak.

Then Gabriel's voice said, "You don't really want to continue feeling upset with Ashley, do you? Look at the turmoil it's causing you. Tell her you're sorry, Jason. You hurt her feelings last week."

Jason didn't want to answer Gabriel. Last week Ashley had said he was crazy for talking to someone who wasn't there, and that is what had caused the argument between them in the first place. So he just waited. He didn't speak to Ashley or Gabriel. Instead, he quietly arranged his project materials the way Mrs. Johnson had asked.

Again, he heard Gabriel's voice. "Go on, Jason. Apologize to Ashley. It certainly can't hurt anything. In fact, you'll feel better if you do."

Jason said nothing for a few minutes more.

Then, knowing once again that his brother was right, he turned to Ashley and said, "Ashley, I'm sorry for what I said. I'm sorry I called your mom fat. I really didn't mean it."

Day 14 ~ Story 14

I Recognize
My Own Best Interest

Jason's class was working on a science project. His teacher, Mrs. Johnson, requested that the students work in pairs consisting of one boy and one girl. Mrs. Johnson asked all the boys to line up on one side of the room, and all the girls to line up on the other side, so they could pair up more easily. Jason had cleverly positioned himself in line so he would be paired with Susie, a girl he really liked.

Just as Mrs. Johnson began pairing up the students, two boys came back into the classroom from the library. Mrs. Johnson quickly shuffled them to the front of the line. Jason couldn't believe his eyes! He was devastated, because he was no longer in the position to be paired up with Susie.

As he began to feel turmoil building up inside, he heard Gabriel saying, "It's okay, Jason. Calm down. Mrs. Johnson did what's best for you."

Jason sat up on his bed and wiped away his tears. He took a few deep breaths and tried to think of something peaceful. In his mind, he saw a bird effortlessly gliding through the air. Below the bird was a stream flowing gently over some rocks. As Jason pictured this in his mind and thought about the peaceful sound of the water flowing, he no longer felt the turmoil of just a few moments before. He had found peace, and he knew exactly what to do with it.

He went downstairs to the living room, and when his parents saw him, they became very quiet. He walked over to his mom, greeted her with a hug and said, "Mom, you are so wonderful! I was just noticing how clean the house is, and was remembering the delicious dinner you cooked last night, and I wanted to tell you that I really appreciate you. There is no mother in the whole world more wonderful than you!"

Jason hugged his mother for a moment longer. She looked down at him and smiled, suddenly feeling very peaceful.

Then he gave his dad a big hug and said, "Dad, you are wonderful, too! You always give me everything I need and want, and you always do fun things with me. I am so happy that you are my dad. You deserve everything in the world, because you are the best dad in the world!"

His father's face lit up with joy, and he said, "Thanks, Jason! I wish you had come in sooner." Then, looking at his wife who was still smiling from the peace her son had brought to her, he added, "We were arguing about nothing at all, honey. Everything is fine now."

The three of them drew together in a warm and happy hug.

"Okay," Mom finally said, "are you guys ready for another delicious meal?"

Jason and his dad both exclaimed, "Yes!" and all three of them headed for the kitchen.

crying. He knelt down with his face in his hands, wishing he could do something about it, but he didn't know what. After a few moments he got up, ran upstairs to his room, and closed the door. Then he threw himself on the bed and began to sob.

Between his sobs, he could hear Gabriel's loving voice.

"Don't cry, my brother." Gabriel murmured.

"But don't you hear them down there?" Jason asked. "They're arguing and blaming each other for not having enough money!"

Gabriel quietly said, "It's okay, my brother. They are going through their own lessons. Dad doesn't understand that he has all the money in the world available to him, and that he could let himself have it just by knowing he has it."

Jason seemed bewildered, so Gabriel continued.

"Some people think they don't deserve to have a lot of money unless they work hard for it. Remember when we talked about how powerful our thoughts are, and how what we believe comes true for us?"

"I remember." Jason said.

"Well," Gabriel said, "if some people believe they have to work hard to receive a lot of money, they won't allow themselves to have as much money as they really want unless they work very hard for it."

Gabriel waited for Jason to think about this for a few moments. When Jason was ready, Gabriel explained some more. "Mom is doing the same thing," he said. "She feels she isn't doing enough work around the house. Because of that, she feels she doesn't deserve the things she wished she had."

Still wanting to do something about the arguing, Jason asked, "Is there anything I can do to help?"

"Yes, Jason, there is," Gabriel answered. "You know how wonderful our parents are. They really need your love right now, because they are feeling like they don't have any love left. But first you must release yourself from the turmoil you are feeling, and open your mind to peace. When you have brought peace to yourself, you will be able to bring peace to them, too."

Day 13 ~ Story 13

I Open My Mind
To Peace

Jason arrived home from school one day and heard noise coming from the living room. His mom and dad were arguing, and shouting at each other. As he got closer to the doorway, he could hear that they were arguing about working too hard and not having enough money.

Jason was upset at hearing his parents arguing like this, and he felt like

As Jason listened to Gabriel's loving voice and began to understand, he thought about releasing the fear. He pictured it as a dark cloud being

sucked up out of him and being replaced with the bright light of peace. He could feel it working. He could feel a sense of peace beginning to come over him.

Seeing this, Gabriel continued. "Just hold your head high and know how powerful you are. Sooner or later, all people are going to discover they also have their own guides—whether it is a loving brother like me, or some other loving spirit who is there for them, as I am for you."

By this time, Jason was totally at peace. He had completely let go of the fear that had overtaken him moments before. "You mean everyone has a guide?" he asked.

Gabriel laughed and replied, "Yes, all people do. Whether they choose to listen or not is up to them, and I am so glad you chose to listen."

treated the other kids. They treated him like someone who was weird or crazy.

After a while, Jason started to be afraid of the way others were treating him. It was difficult to be around them. He would try to act in a way they considered to be normal, but it wasn't easy, because he was often talking to Gabriel.

One afternoon, as Jason was walking home from school, he saw some other kids staring and pointing at him from across the street. Right away he became fearful. Hairs stood up on the back of his neck. Then he heard Gabriel's voice in his mind, asking, "My brother, why are you so afraid?"

"People think I am weird." Jason whispered.

"No, my brother, they don't think you are weird," Gabriel replied. "They may treat you different from the way they treat the other kids, but it is only that they recognize how powerful you are. They know you are communicating with someone they can't see."

"Then where is this fear coming from?"

Gabriel explained, "You are fearful because you don't understand why some people treat you differently. You are the one who has decided the reason is fearful, and so you are afraid. You believe these people don't like you, but the truth is they like you a lot. They just don't understand you, Jason. Because they are not in touch with their inner guides who could teach them to understand and could bring them a sense of peace about it, they treat you differently. Release the fear, my brother. It has no place in your mind."

Day 12 ~ Story 12

I Release All Fear

There was a story going around school about Jason being very powerful and having some kind of guide with him all the time. Some kids were excited about the idea and wanted to be close to Jason, but others didn't understand, and they kept distant from him. Because they often saw him talking to someone they couldn't see, they treated him different from the way they

his heart. He couldn't help but smile as he remembered what Gabriel had told him about gifts of kindness.

By the end of the day, Jason had found places to give away all the gifts he had taken with him that day—the gifts in his backpack and the gifts in his heart. When he lay down to sleep that night, he thought about all the giving he had done, and felt a strong sense of peace, love, and joy within. It felt as if he were floating high in the sky on a cloud, with the gentle warmth of the sun caressing him.

He thanked Gabriel for the miracle of his never–ending guidance.

pulled out a fuzzy teddy bear that one of his classmates had given him.

"Mom, I love you!" he said. "I would like you to have this teddy bear because you're such a wonderful mom."

His mother's face lit up. She took the teddy bear, hugged her son, and watched him run off to school.

Along the way, Jason walked by a house where a little boy about five years old was sitting on the front lawn. "Where's your mom, Tyler?" Jason called out.

The boy replied, "She's coming with some cookies."

Jason knelt down on the ground where he was sitting. "Whatcha doing?" he asked.

Tyler said, "I'm tryin' to tie my shoes, but it's not workin'. I wanted to surprise Mommy."

Jason asked, "Can you show me how you do it?"

"Okay." Tyler said.

As Jason watched the boy tie his shoe, he noticed one thing Tyler was doing wrong. "I think it goes like this," he said. Then he gently took the boy's fingers, guiding them through the correct motions. "You put the loop through this way."

"Oh." Tyler said.

"Now why don't you try it with the other shoe." Jason suggested.

Tyler carefully followed Jason's direction and successfully tied his other shoe. "I did it! I did it by myself!" he screamed joyfully.

Jason smiled and stood up as he heard Tyler's mom from inside the house.

"Tyler," she called out, "is everything okay?"

Tyler jumped up and ran toward the house, yelling, "Mommy! I did it! I did it!" Before he reached the front door, he turned back and called out, "Thanks, Jason!" Then he disappeared inside.

As Jason continued on to school, he noticed a warm feeling of love inside

"I am here, my brother," Gabriel answered. "How may I help you?"

"Well," Jason said, "I'm bewildered. I am so thankful to have received all these wonderful gifts, but there is no way I could possibly use all of them. There are so many!"

Gabriel softly replied, "This is a good time for you to learn the lesson of giving to others, Jason."

"Giving to others? How does that fit in?"

"It is important for you to give as you receive," Gabriel said. "If you hold on to everything and keep it to yourself, much of it will just sit there unused, and you won't even know that you have it. Keep what you will use, Jason, and give the rest of it away. In doing this, you will be reminded that you have so many wonderful things."

"But these are my things," Jason interrupted. "They were given to me! How can I just give them to somebody else?"

"That they are your things is what makes it possible for you to give them away," Gabriel explained. "When you receive something, it becomes yours—but you really know that you have something when you give it away. You certainly can't give something away that you don't have."

"Okay, I understand about gifts that are things," Jason said. "But what if it's not a gift like a toy or a game, but it's a gift of kindness that is given to me? Like when people help me in school, or cook for me, or take me to fun places. Can I give away gifts of kindness, too?"

"Absolutely!" Gabriel exclaimed. He was glad his brother had quickly understood that giving includes more than objects. "Gifts of kindness are the best to receive, and they are also the best to give. In receiving gifts of kindness and in giving gifts of kindness, your heart is filled with love."

Jason was so excited! Now he couldn't wait to see how it would feel to give away some of the wonderful things he had received. Gabriel had told him to look around for people who could use some joy and laughter, so he filled his backpack with gifts, and decided to give them all away by the end of the day.

He gave the first gift to his mother, who was looking gloomy at the breakfast table. On his way to the door, he reached into his backpack and

Day 11 ~ Story 11

I Give As I Receive

The next day, Jason looked around his room at all the gifts he had been receiving. He thought about how effortless his life had become, now that everyone was always offering to help him and do things for him.

He looked around and wondered, "What am I going to do with all these gifts?!" Then he called out quietly, "Gabriel, are you here?"

"It's really that easy for everyone," Jason said. "Nobody has to do anything. Just being open to receive is enough."

Gabriel was always delighted when his brother understood, and he replied with joy. "You're absolutely right! And that's also the reason you can hear me, Jason. If you were not open to receive my guidance, I wouldn't be able to communicate with you the way I have been since making my transition."

Jason was glad that he was open to receive, because it allowed him to communicate with his brother. He would always be thankful for that miracle.

thanked Brittany with a smile.

As he started at the box in his hand, he began to feel uncomfortable. He remembered Gabriel's words, "You deserve it," and had learned the lesson well. He really understood that he truly deserved all the wonderful things that came into his life, but now there was something else that bothered him.

Gabriel knew how Jason was feeling at that moment. He was always there when his brother needed him. "What's wrong, Jason?" he asked.

"Another gift." his brother said quietly.

"I noticed," Gabriel replied. "Isn't it wonderful?"

"Well, yes," Jason said, "it's wonderful for me, and I know I deserve it— but Gabriel, what about everybody else? Why am I so special? Why doesn't everybody deserve wonderful things?"

"My brother," Gabriel said, "everybody else does deserve wonderful things!"

"But then, why don't all people constantly have wonderful things happening in their lives, the way I have them happening?" Jason asked. "I don't even do anything for these things; they just happen to me!"

"You don't have to do anything, except to be open to receive," Gabriel explained. "It's very important for all people to know they deserve wonderful things, and to be open to receive them. Most people are not open to receive, and so they don't receive. It's that simple."

Jason looked bewildered, so Gabriel explained further. "It's like being in a room with the door closed. On the other side of the door is a wonderland where you can have gifts of every kind, all the joy and love you could imagine, and every possible happy experience you might think of. Being open to receive is like opening the door and simply stepping through, into that wonderland."

Jason was listening carefully, and so Gabriel continued. "When you are not open to receive, it's like standing in front of the closed door and not opening it. On the other side are all these wonderful things, but you can't have them if you don't open the door. When all people are open to receive the way you have become, they will receive the same way that you do."

Day 10 ~ Story 10

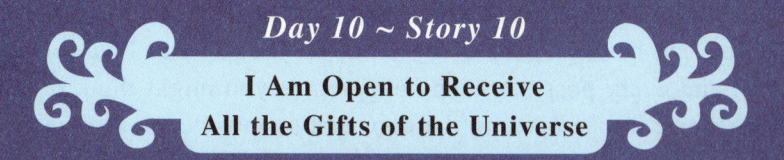

I Am Open to Receive All the Gifts of the Universe

The following week, as Jason was leaving his classroom, a classmate named Brittany walked over to him with a small box in her hand. She held it out him and said, "Jason, I have a gift for you."

This was the third time in a week that one of his classmates had given him a gift, so he was getting pretty good at accepting them. He took the box and

cheers up and starts laughing along with me."

"Exactly," Gabriel said. "When people are around you, they feel your joy and love within themselves—it is a gift from you to them, and so they contribute joy and love back to you. Sometimes the joy and love can be a smile, sometimes it is words, sometimes it might be help where you think you would like help, and sometimes it is a thing—a present. They are all wonderful gifts being contributed to you. So, now do you understand that you do deserve all the wonderful contributions from everyone?"

Jason mumbled, "Well, maybe I do."

Quickly Gabriel said, "It's more than 'maybe', Jason. You definitely do! And it's very important to know and keep reminding yourself that you do deserve wonderful things. Remember when we talked about how powerful your thoughts are?"

"I remember." Jason said.

"Well, you don't want to get in the habit of thinking you don't deserve wonderful things, do you?"

Gabriel asked.

Jason thought about this for a moment. Gabriel was telling him that if he started believing he didn't deserve wonderful things, then he would never receive wonderful things.

He let this sink deeply into his mind until he finally understood. "You are absolutely right," he told Gabriel. "I am a wonderful person, and I deserve all the wonderful things that come to me. We all deserve all the wonderful things that come to us!"

With this understanding, Jason decided he would never again doubt that he truly did deserve all the contributions from everyone in his life.

Day 9 ~ Story 9

I Deserve Prosperity

After more than a week of miracles, Jason was becoming concerned again. He still didn't fully understand why everyone was doing so much to contribute to him. He wondered if he really deserved all the gifts and help that everyone was always offering.

Gabriel quickly came to Jason's rescue and assured his brother that he really did deserve everyone's contributions. Then Gabriel told him why.

"My beloved Jason," Gabriel began, "you are such a wonderful person! You are always laughing—you are so full of joy and love that people can't help but love you!"

Jason thought about this and said, "Well, I guess that's true—I have noticed that when I get around someone who is in a bad mood, the person suddenly being joyous.

It wasn't long before everyone wanted to be near Jason. There seemed to be something magical about him—whenever others were around him, they felt the same carefree joy that he felt.

People loved giving Jason gifts and contributing to him in every way. At school, his classmates gave him toys and games and extra snacks at lunch, his teachers always offered their help with his school work, and all the team captains in P.E. class wanted to choose him for their teams.

And at home, his mom cooked his favorite dinners and took him shopping whenever he asked, and his dad often took him to the park to shoot baskets, which was one of his favorite things to do.

Jason felt so very loved. He constantly thanked Gabriel and everyone else for their contributions to him.

On one afternoon, as Jason was walking home from school, he asked Gabriel, "How come everyone wants to give me things all the time?"

"Well, maybe because you are a nice guy and everybody knows that," Gabriel said.

Jason walked without speaking for a while, as he thought about Gabriel's answer. Finally he asked, "You don't think they feel sorry for me since you are gone, do you?"

"No, not at all," Gabriel answered. "They like to give you things because first, you are grateful for everything, and second, you are always happy and joyous. That makes everyone feel that they would like to contribute to you."

Jason smiled and said, "I think I am beginning to understand."

Day 8 ~ Story 8

**Everyone Wishes
To Contribute to Me**

Jason was feeling so very prosperous! Lately, whatever he desired just seemed to show up in his life, effortlessly. It was almost as if he had his very own genie!

Knowing that he did not have to want, or worry, or wonder, gave him such a feeling of freedom that he constantly walked around laughing and

With a big grin and a bigger "thank you", Jason accepted the twenty dollar bill and ran off toward home.

At dinner that evening, he told his mom and dad about all the things that had happened to him that day, and about how he had received exactly enough money to buy the game he had wished for. He never mentioned Gabriel's help, but told his parents what he had learned.

"Whenever I wish for something, I know it will somehow be given to me if I am really supposed to have it. All I have to do is wish for something, and then forget about the wish—and miracles happen!"

Jason's mom and dad noticed the joy and confidence shining in his face, and they clearly understood how very prosperous he was.

turned to him.

"Hi there, young fella," he said. "I guess you're probably wondering what I'm doing, aren't you."

"Well—kind of." Jason said.

The man pointed into the tree. "My Boodles—you know, my kitten—my favorite kitten in the whole world is up there. She was running from a big German shepherd, and it chased her right up into this tree!"

Jason looked up through the tree branches and saw the cat. "It's not so very high," he said. "Can't she just jump down?"

"I think she probably could, but she's too scared," the man said.

Jason, who had climbed all the trees in his own yard many times, said, "I bet I could get her down for you."

The man's eyes sparkled with hope. "Do you really think so?"

"Yeah," Jason said as he dropped his backpack on the grass. "I'm pretty good at climbing trees."

He grabbed a branch and lifted himself up into the tree. Within two minutes he had scooped Boodles up, tucked him into his shirt, climbed back down the tree, and returned safely to the ground. He handed the kitten to its owner, noticing tears of joy in the man's eyes.

"Oh, I don't know how to thank you," he said. "Boodles is all I have left in the world."

"Oh, it's okay," Jason said. "It was pretty easy."

He reached down to pick up his backpack, so he could continue on his way home. At the same time, the man reached into his pocket, pulled out his wallet, and held put a crisp twenty dollar bill.

"Please take this money and buy yourself something fun!" he said.

Jason just stood there, staring at the money.

The man laughed, "Please, son, take the money. I really want you to have it!"

Leaning down to pick up the ball, Jason noticed a piece of green paper that was stuck in the fence, flapping in the breeze. He drew closer for a better look, and then jumped with joy to see that it was actually a ten dollar bill! Now he had fifteen dollars toward his new game!

At the end of the school day he walked home with a bounce in his step, feeling very, very prosperous. How wonderful it was to know that whenever he wished to have money, he would receive it immediately with Gabriel's help.

When he was a few blocks from home, he passed a man about his grandpa's age. The man was standing in his yard, talking to a tree. Jason was curious, so he moved closer. The man continued his tree talk, and what Jason heard was, "Come on, Boodles—climb down to see your daddy. Daddy has some treats for you, Boodles."

As Jason moved even closer, to get a better look up into the tree, the man

me."

Jason was confused. "What do you mean, follow you?" he asked. "How can I follow you when I can't even see you?"

"I mean, just go where I direct you," Gabriel said, "and by the end of the day you will have enough money to buy your game."

"Really?" Jason asked in disbelief. He was doubtful at first, but he had learned that anything Gabriel told him always seemed to turn out to be true. Little by little, he became more excited by the idea. Finally he said, "Okay, Gabriel—you guide me, and I will follow you."

As the lunch bell rang, Gabriel said to Jason, "How about stopping in the bathroom to wash your hands before lunch?"

"That's a good idea," Jason said. He walked into the boy's lavatory and headed for the sink.

"What's under that sink?" Gabriel asked.

Looking down, Jason saw a crumpled five dollar bill in the corner. He picked it up, smoothed it out, and stared at it. "You're kidding me," he giggled. "You mean it's just that easy?"

Gabriel was delighted at his beloved brother's joy. "Yes!" he exclaimed. "It's just that easy!"

Jason ran off to the cafeteria, ate lunch with his best friend, and went out to shoot some baskets before lunch period ended. After a few minutes of shooting and dribbling back and forth, Jason shot a basket so high that the ball went over the backboard and landed by the schoolyard fence. He ran to get the ball.

"Jason—what's that blowing against the fence?" Gabriel asked.

Day 7 ~ Story 7

I Am Very Prosperous

The first time it happened, Jason was in class waiting for the lunch bell to ring. He was thinking out loud about a new video game he wanted, and Gabriel suddenly asked him how much the game would cost. Jason told Gabriel the game would cost thirty-five dollars.

"If that is what you desire, then you've got it," Gabriel said. "Just follow

Change his thoughts?" Jason asked, "What do you mean?"

"If he continues having these dark thoughts, he really will get fired," Gabriel explained. "But it won't be because his boss doesn't like him, it will be because our thoughts are so powerful that whatever we believe comes true for us."

"Okay, Gabriel," Jason said. "I'll do whatever I can, to help." He walked over to his father and said, "Dad, I know you are worried about getting fired, but do you think you could try to change your mind about the situation?"

His parents looked at each other in surprise. "Change my mind? What do you mean, Jason?" his dad asked.

Jason explained. "Somebody once told me our thoughts are so powerful that whatever we believe will happen does actually happen. So if you changed your mind and stared thinking you are doing a great job at work and your boss really appreciates you, you'll see that he really does appreciate you. Then you will keep your job as long as you wish."

His mom and dad looked at each other again, surprised to hear him saying such grown-up things. Dad pulled Jason toward him, and sat him on him lap. "You're growing up fast, son! Do they teach you these things in school?"

Before Jason could answer, his mom interrupted. "He's right, honey! What he says makes sense. If you change your attitude about the situation, we'll all feel much better."

Jason's dad thought carefully about what his son had told him, and what his wife had just said. Finally he agreed. "Yes," he said, "you are both right. I will change my attitude. At the very least, I won't have to worry so much."

So, from that day on, his dad made sure he had thoughts that he was doing an excellent job, and that his boss really appreciated him. And it wasn't long before his boss showed him how much he was appreciated, by paying him more money.

Day 6 ~ Story 6

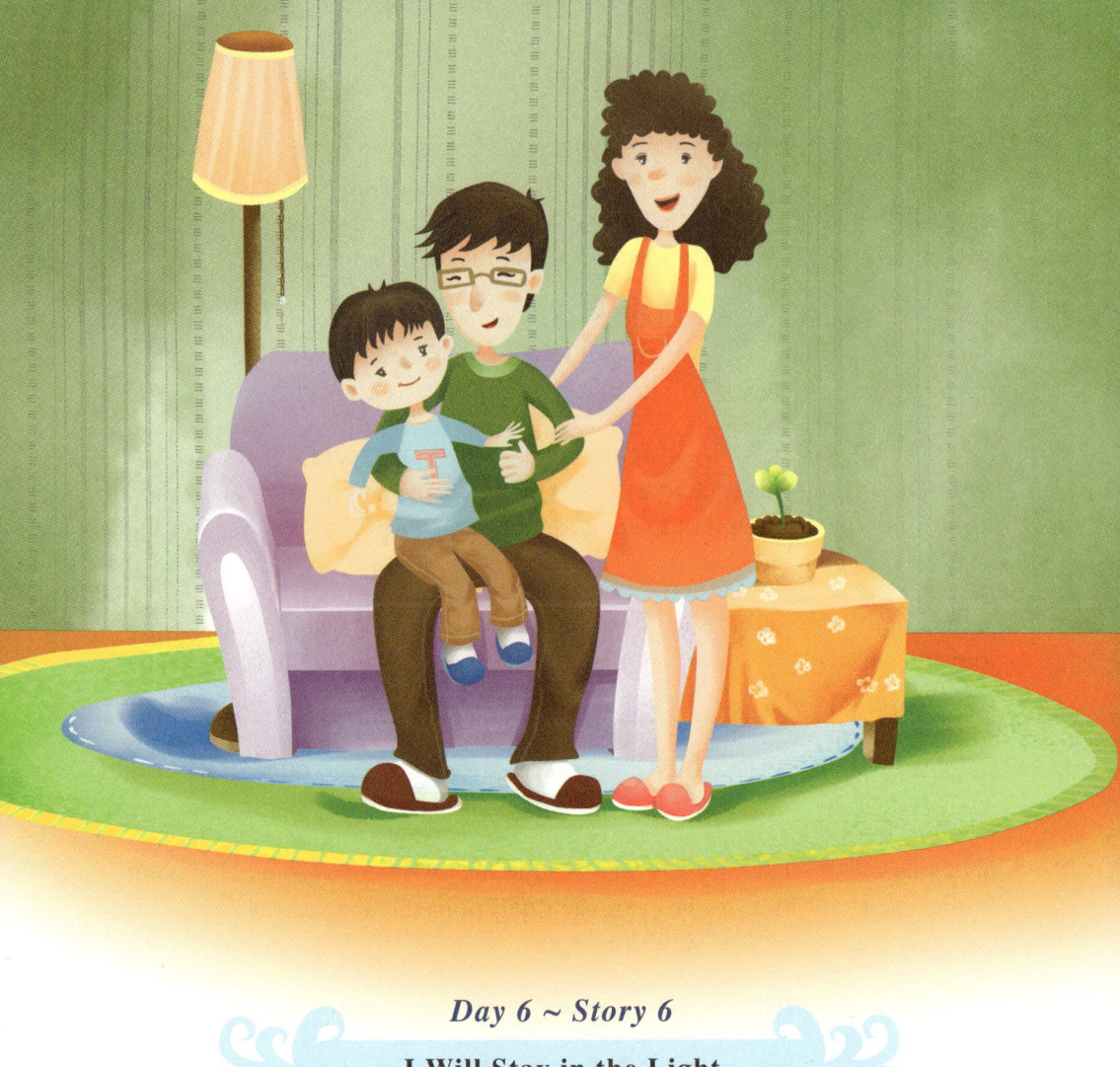

I Will Stay in the Light

The next morning, as Jason was heading into the kitchen to eat breakfast, he heard his parents discussing his dad's job.

"I think I am going to get fired," Dad said in a worried voice. "I'm afraid that I haven't been doing a very good job at work, and that my boss is unhappy with me."

Jason's mom was quiet, but she also appeared to be worried.

At this moment Jason heard Gabriel say, "Jason, you have to help change our father's thoughts and bring light and peace to his mind."

"You must look within yourself, Jason," Gabriel answered. "The right answers are there. You must let go of all worry about not being good enough and not knowing the right answers. You have studied enough. Just open your mind to receive the right answers, and they will come to you."

Jason still could not relax. He was so worried! "Oh please, Gabriel," he begged, "can't you just look around for the smartest kids and find the right answers for me? Please?"

"If I do that, Jason, you will think the answers came from outside of you, and you will not understand that they are already within you. Just relax. Relax and allow your mind to think. Let it open to what it knows, and the answers will come to you."

Jason could see that he wasn't going to be able to talk Gabriel into giving him the answers, and he knew that Gabriel had always guided him in the right direction before, so he decided to trust him. After a few moments of trusting, he no longer felt worried—he was wrapped up in a soft blanket of peace and quietness.

Smiling with confidence, Jason began reading the questions on the test, believing all the right answers were within his own mind, just as his loving brother had told him. As he read each question, the answers came to him easily, and he wrote them down.

"Thank you, Gabriel," he said to himself each time he wrote an answer.

"Thank you for showing me that the answers are all within my own mind." Jason's joy grew even more the next day when he saw the excellent grade on his test.

Day 5 ~ Story 5

I Am Willing To See
The Light

A few days later, Jason was having a test at school. He was nervous because he felt he had not studied enough to get a good grade, but he knew he could get help from his brother.

"Gabriel!" he said quietly, "Look around the classroom to see who has the right answers. As you find the answers, give them to me! Okay?"

"Oh Gabriel," he whispered, "there is a horrible man here in my room, and he is going to attack me! Please help!"

"Jason—there is no one in your room except us," Gabriel said.

"Oh, but there is someone else here," Jason whispered. "I can see him! I can see him!"

"My loving brother," Gabriel said in a soothing voice, "there is a string from your pajama hood hanging in front of your eyes. That is what you are seeing as a monster."

Jason slowly reached his hand up to his eyes. Gently touching the string that was hanging there, he realized Gabriel's words were true, and he breathed a sigh of relief.

Gabriel continued in a loving tone, "You had a nightmare, my brother, and in your fear you gave a harmless string the power of a monster. What you have seen here doesn't have any real meaning. How can a string be a monster? It was only your decision about it that made it seem that way to you. The meaning you gave it has nothing to do with reality. Now, are you still afraid?"

Jason settled back on his pillow and said, "No, Gabriel, I'm not afraid anymore."

"Good," Gabriel replied. "As soon as you saw the truth, you realized that you were safe, and that nothing was going to hurt you. I want you to remember something very important. What you think you see isn't always real. Ask me the meaning of what you see, and I will show you."

Jason was very excited to hear this. "Instead of trying to figure out what something means, I should just ask you? And you will show me its real meaning? And I won't make any more scary mistakes about what I am seeing?"

"That's right, my brother," Gabriel said. "Let me show you the real meaning of everything, and you will never be afraid again!"

Jason laughed. "It's a deal!"

Day 4 ~ Story 4

I Do Not Know
The Real Meaning
Of What I See

One night Jason had a nightmare and woke up screaming. As he opened his eyes, he saw the shadowy figure of a man hiding by the door.

He was very scared, so he squeezed his eyes tightly shut, hoping the man would think he was still asleep, and would go away. When he opened his eyes again for a peek, he saw the shadow man moving very quickly around the room.

Jason was just about to scream for his mom or dad to come in and save him, when he remembered something important. "Gabriel is always with me!" he thought to himself. "I'll call to him, in my mind!"

The moment he called out to Gabriel, he heard a soft voice respond. "What is the matter, my loving brother? Why are you calling for me?"

one was there.

"Is that you, Gabriel?" he asked. He could not hear Gabriel's voice, but he felt his shoulder being touched again in response. It seemed his brother was trying to draw him away from the scene of the fight.

Jason walked away from the fight and looked in the opposite direction, where he noticed two other kids sitting in the grass, sharing lunch, and laughing together. The turmoil he had felt just moments before began to fade. A sense of joy came over him as he watched the two friends eating lunch.

Faintly, and then louder and more clearly, Jason began to hear Gabriel's voice again.

"Oh, Gabriel," he said, "I'm so glad I can hear you again! I knew you were with me before, but I couldn't hear your voice."

"Whenever you are upset or in turmoil of any kind, you are so full of your own emotion that you cannot hear me," Gabriel responded. "It is very important for you to be aware of what you are looking at. When you look at things that upset you, the turmoil will get in the way of my voice and guidance. Did you notice how quickly you were able to hear me when you began watching the two friends eating lunch and being joyous?"

"Yes, you're right," Jason said. "Once I looked at something peaceful and joyous instead of something full of turmoil, I could hear you again! From now on, I will always pay close attention to what I am looking at. I will turn away from any situation that brings me turmoil, and will only look at situations that bring me joy and peace."

Day 3 ~ Story 3

I Am Aware of What I see

One afternoon as Jason was heading toward the cafeteria for lunch, he saw two of his classmates arguing and shoving each other over some nonsense about homework. He could not take his eyes off the fight scene, but he also felt a great deal of turmoil from looking at it.

Suddenly he felt someone touching his shoulder. When he turned around, no

One day as Jason was leaving his classroom, he passed by a teacher in the hallway. The teacher stopped him and began to cry.

"Oh Jason," she said, "I am so sorry about what happened to your brother. I know you must miss him so much—you must be very sad—."

As Jason listened to the teacher, he could feel himself getting ready to cry. But then he heard Gabriel's voice, saying, "Brother, don't listen to these things that are not true. The teacher doesn't know that I am with you, but you do. You know I am here, so don't believe the stories other people tell you just because they believe them to be true."

Jason immediately pulled himself back together. He smiled and thanked the teacher for her words, saying that he had to get to his classroom.

As he ran down the hallway remembering the truth about his brother, he felt a sense of peace flow over him. He was so glad that he had not allowed himself to become upset by someone else's untrue belief.

Watching Jason leave, the teacher was amazed at how quickly the boy's expression had changed. For a moment he had looked as though he were going to cry, but then a big smile had lighted up his face, and he had run down the hall very joyfully.

As Jason walked home from school later that day, he asked Gabriel, "How long will I have to listen to other people's nonsense?"

Gabriel explained, "The less attention you give to other people's untrue beliefs, the sooner people will stop talking to you about them. Simply let go of their words, Jason. Do not listen to them."

Day 2 ~ Story 2

I Notice What I Hear

During the next few days, Jason found himself being affected by what other kids and teachers at school were saying about his brother's transition, No one understood that Gabriel was still alive.

They all believed that, because he was no longer in his body, he was dead.

story? I am still alive and with you—so lighten up and start having fun!"

Jason finished tying his shoelace, stood up, and smiled at his friend. "Forget about the story, Tom.. We are here to have fun—let's go and shoot some baskets!" The two boys gave each other a high-five, and ran toward the basketball courts.

As they were playing basketball, Tome stopped, looked at Jason, and said, "I can believe that you are not very upset about your brother."

Jason found himself feeling upset again, and was about to go back to the story and drama of it, when he heard Gabriel's voice again. "Hold it, Jason. Let it go—please let it go. Did you forget that I am here with you? Please get back to the joy of playing, and remember what is really going on."

Jason turned to Tom and said, "Hey, I came here to shoot some baskets so I don't have to think about that for awhile. Do you mind?"

Tom put his hands up, saying, "Okay, okay, I will not talk about it anymore. Let's play basketball."

The two friends got back to the joy of the moment and shot baskets until the school bell rang.

Day 1~ Story 1

I Watch What I Say

The next morning, Jason went to school early, so he could play basketball before the day began. As he walked through the schoolyard, he saw his best friend, Tom.

"Hey, Jason, what's happening?" Tom asked.

Trying not to cry, Jason began to tell Tom the story of his brother's tragic accident. Halfway through the story, he heard Gabriel's voice interrupting him.

"Jason, stop it!" Gabriel said.

Jason bent down to tie his shoe so he could listen to his brother.

"Wasn't it upsetting enough to live through the experience once?" Gabriel asked. "Now that you know I really did not die, do you have to tell this

"I can't wait to tell Mom and Dad that you are still with me," he said. "They will be so happy!"

But Gabriel answered quickly, "No, you can not tell our parents, because you are the only one who can hear me. My promise was to you, Jason. I did not have the agreement with Mom and Dad."

Giving it one more try, Jason said, "But this is so cool, Gabriel! We should tell other people about it!"

"No, Jason," Gabriel answered. "This is only between you and me."

Jason sat quietly, thinking about this agreement, and about his brother. "How long are you going to be here?" he asked.

"As long as you wish for me to be with you," Gabriel answered.

When Jason went downstairs and saw how sad his parents were, he wanted to let them know that Gabriel was really still with him—but Gabriel had made him promise not to tell anyone. Jason knew it was important to keep his word, and he knew that Gabriel trusted him to do that.

So, he would trust Gabriel, and know that his brother must have an important reason for this pact.

As he watched his mom and dad quietly crying, he heard Gabriel's voice saying, "It's okay, Jason —we will tell them someday. Thank you for keeping your word. Our word is very powerful, and it is very important for everyone to keep his word."

And so it begins—

NOTE

The author has created Gabriel and Jason to help the reader better understand the messages presented in each story. The reader does not have to have known someone who has made a "transition" in order to understand the stories and to begin using the ideas presented, in his or her daily life.

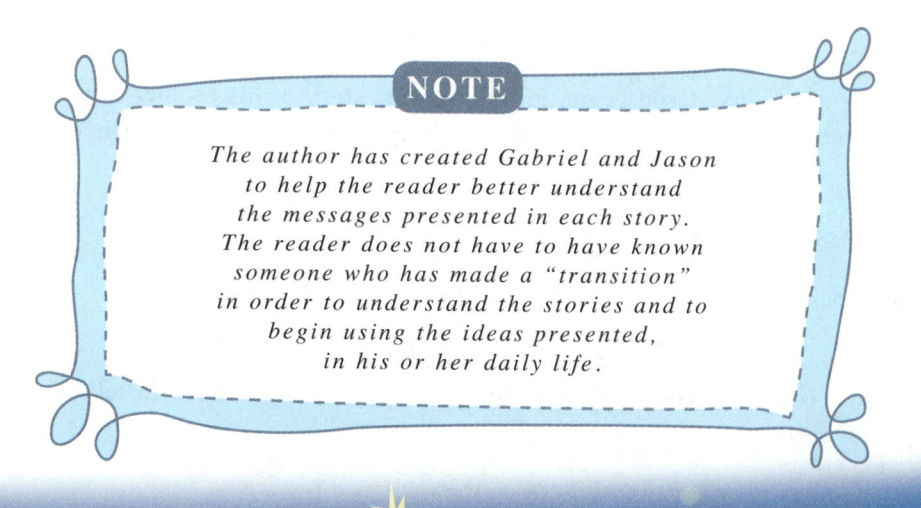

telling the boys, "If you always remember the truth about who you really are and why you are here, your lives together will always be joyous and loving."

Jason and Gabriel now understood. Feeling a strong sense of joy and love for each other, they continued discussing what their father had told them, both knowing deep down inside that it was the truth.

"You know, Gabriel," Jason said, "I don't know which one of us will make our transition first, but if you do, I want you to promise me one thing. Promise that you will stay with me, and guide me for as long as I am in this body."

Gabriel smiled at his brother. "I will promise you, as long as you promise me the same thing." he said.

At that, the brothers laughed, shook hands, hugged each other, and agreed they would never forget their promise.

Shortly after this day of discovery, Gabriel was involved in what appeared to be a tragic accident, and he made his transition.

It was a sad moment for the whole family, but it was especially sad for Jason. Jason felt a great sense of loss, because he had become so close to his brother Gabriel, and had truly learned to see Gabriel as his friend, brother, and guide.

As Jason sat in his room, sadly looking at some of the toys and games he and Gabriel had played with together, he suddenly heard a voice. He looked around the room, but nobody was there.

Again he heard the voice, and this time it was shouting, "I am still here! I did not leave you!"

Jason looked around again, and still saw no one. Suspiciously, he asked the voice, "Who are you? Is somebody hiding in here?"

The voice replied, "Don't be afraid—it's me—it's Gabriel. I am keeping my promise. Just listen to me and do what I guide you to do, and we will both be happy."

Jason could still see no one, but he could hear Gabriel's voice very clearly in his mind. Jason was excited. He hadn't lost his brother after all!

Gabriel and Jason looked at each other. They smiled at this idea. Not fully understanding it, the two looked seriously at their father and said, "Please tell us more."

Dad sat down with the two boys and continued to explain.

"The body is not really who we are," he said. "The truth is that we are all spirits who choose to come to this planet to have experiences that help us learn and grow. We choose our family and loved ones, we choose the lessons we would like to learn, and we even choose who we would like to help us learn these lessons."

"As spirits, we use the body as a vehicle, just like a car. Our body takes us around this planet to different places, so we can communicate with the other spirits who are also in bodies."

He told the boys that they had chosen to be two brothers called Jason and Gabriel in this life, so they could be together to help each other learn and grow. He also told them that there is no death, because spirits can never die.

"When a body loses its life," he continued, "it only appears that it has died. What really happens is that the spirits has reached its highest learning and growth possible in that body, so it simply leaves the body and moves on to whatever other experiences it chooses. This is called a transition."

As Dad stood up to go and get ready for work, he ended his explanation by

My Guiding Spirit
— and so it begins

In an ordinary neighborhood just like any other, there were a loving father and mother of two young sons—Gabriel, who was 11 years old, and Jason, who was 10 years old. Quite often, just like other brothers, the two boys would have arguments and disagreements.

Early one morning, as the boys were arguing, their dad pulled both of them aside and asked, "Do you know why you two are arguing?"

Both Jason and Gabriel answered at the same time, each blaming the other for stealing favorite games or toys, and grabbing food.

Their dad listened to them for a while and then said, "No, those are not your real reasons for arguing. There is only one real reason, and it is that you both have forgotten who you are and why you are here. You do not remember that before you came into these bodies, you had such a strong love for each other that you chose to come here to Earth as brothers, to help one another."

The Stories

When you have Love in your heart,

fear will be gone—

So relax and be happy

How To Enjoy This Book

The thirty stories in this book are based upon the thirty lessons of Absolutely Effortless Prosperity Book I. The stories in Effortless Prosperity for Youths have been written to get young boys and girls in touch with the beauty of their innocence, and to open them to respect for themselves, respect and love for their parents, and also respect and love for every living thing on this planet.

The book is designed to be read one story a day, which has one lesson a day. The number on each story corresponds to the day of the month. If there is an extra day in the month, you can choose one of your favorite stories to read for that day.

It is recommended to read the daily story upon waking up in the morning, and again at bedtime, to bring happy, joyous, and loving dreams. Whatever the mind focuses on, the mind goes toward. It is that simple. In doing this, you will open your eyes, mind and heart to all the miracles which are available to you every day, at every moment.

Then, in writing your thoughts and miracles in the Daily Journal provided for you in this book, you will also concrete each lesson and open yourself up even more to seeing all the miracles in your life.

Open to receive and acknowledge the miracles of joy, peace, love, friendship, health and prosperity in your daily life, and share them with your family and friends. This will ensure the best results in thirty days.

Message from Bijan

To all my wonderful young friends —

you are the future of this planet. Stay in peace and listen to your intuition, your guides, and your angels.

You don't have to lose anyone in your family to have guides; you already have wonderful guides within you, who will help you in making the best choice of what to do at every moment.

Your most powerful guides are your mom and dad. Always follow their advice, and always remember—whether you see it or not, they do love you more than you can imagine at this time. The only way you will know how much they love you will be when you have a child of your own.

I wish you all the best, now and in the future.

Love, light, and happiness always—from your friend,

Prosperity

is the ability to be open to receive

all the gifts the universe has to offer.

It is our natural state of being

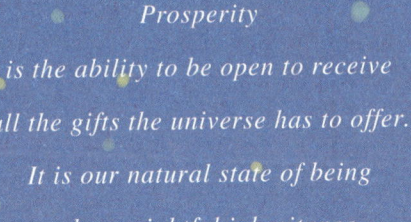

and our rightful inheritance.

Prosperity is much more than money.

It also means excellent health,

unlimited joy, wonderful relationships,

and total peace.

When children feel prosperous,

they know that they are worthy and deserving

of everything wonderful in this world.

Therefore, they can give up their beliefs of

limitation and scarcity and open themselves up

to a great and successful future – a future filled

with so much joy, peace and wellbeing.

Introduction

30-Day Miracle Journal *107*

Day 1 ~ Story 1   /108

Day 2 ~ Story 2   /108

Day 3 ~ Story 3   /108

Day 4 ~ Story 4   /109

Day 5 ~ Story 5   /109

Day 6 ~ Story 6   /109

Day 7 ~ Story 7   /110

Day 8 ~ Story 8   /110

Day 9 ~ Story 9   /110

Day 10 ~ Story 10   /111

Day 11 ~ Story 11   /111

Day 12 ~ Story 12   /111

Day 13 ~ Story 13   /112

Day 14 ~ Story 14   /112

Day 15 ~ Story 15   /112

Day 16 ~ Story 16   /113

Day 17 ~ Story 17   /113

Day 18 ~ Story 18   /113

Day 19 ~ Story 19   /114

Day 20 ~ Story 20   /114

Day 21 ~ Story 21   /114

Day 22 ~ Story 22   /115

Day 23 ~ Story 23   /115

Day 24 ~ Story 24   /115

Day 25 ~ Story 25   /116

Day 26 ~ Story 26   /116

Day 27 ~ Story 27   /116

Day 28 ~ Story 28   /117

Day 29 ~ Story 29   /117

Day 30 ~ Story 30   /117

Epilogue *118*

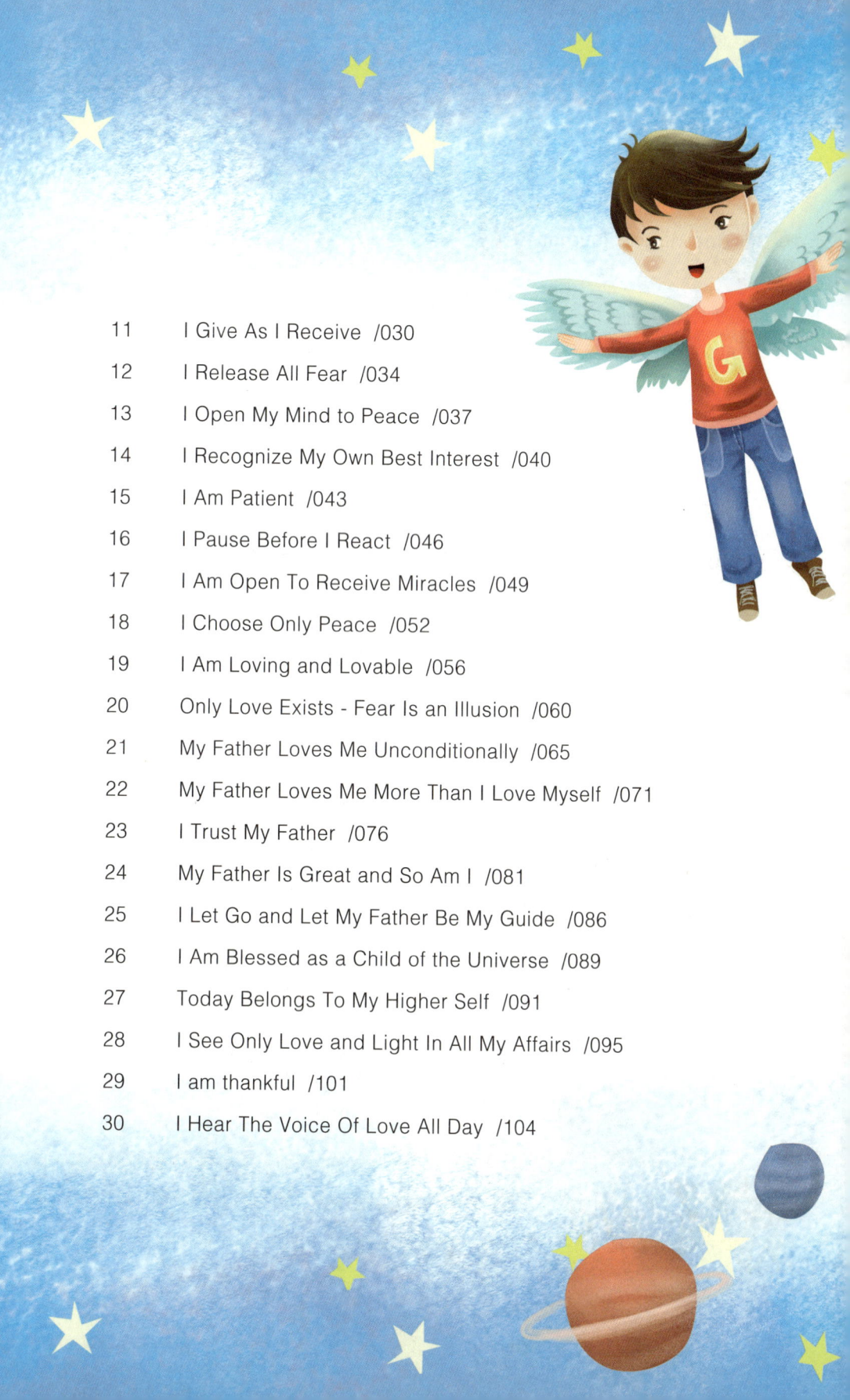

11	I Give As I Receive /030
12	I Release All Fear /034
13	I Open My Mind to Peace /037
14	I Recognize My Own Best Interest /040
15	I Am Patient /043
16	I Pause Before I React /046
17	I Am Open To Receive Miracles /049
18	I Choose Only Peace /052
19	I Am Loving and Lovable /056
20	Only Love Exists - Fear Is an Illusion /060
21	My Father Loves Me Unconditionally /065
22	My Father Loves Me More Than I Love Myself /071
23	I Trust My Father /076
24	My Father Is Great and So Am I /081
25	I Let Go and Let My Father Be My Guide /086
26	I Am Blessed as a Child of the Universe /089
27	Today Belongs To My Higher Self /091
28	I See Only Love and Light In All My Affairs /095
29	I am thankful /101
30	I Hear The Voice Of Love All Day /104

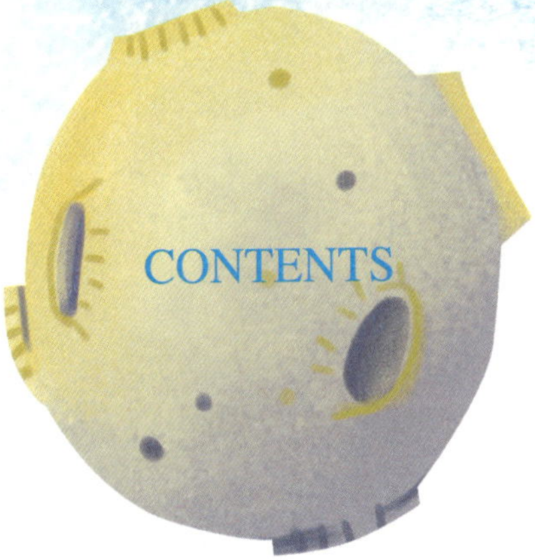

CONTENTS

Introduction *1*

Message from Bijan /3

How To Enjoy This Book /4

The Stories *001*

My Guiding Spirit—And So It Continues /002

1   I Watch What I Say /006

2   I Notice What I Hear /008

3   I Am Aware of What I See /010

4   I Do Not Know the Real Meaning Of What I See /012

5   I Am Willing To See the Light /014

6   I Will Stay in the Light /016

7   I Am Very Prosperous /018

8   Everyone Wishes To Contribute to Me /023

9   I Deserve Prosperity /025

10   I Am Open To Receive All the Gifts of the Universe /027

Two or more children
who are vigilant for the light
are much more powerful
than hundreds of people
living in darkness.

I dedicate this book to all my young brothers
and sisters all over this planet.
You are beautiful souls
and the wonderful adults of our future.
Play and have fun in life,
and life will have fun with you.
Thank you for being on this planet with me.
I love you!

MY GUIDING SPIRIT 1

Absolutely Effortless Prosperity For Youths

Bijan Anjomi